THE BEAUTY OF
BRITAIN
& IRELAND

THE BEAUTY OF BRITAIN AND IRELAND

JOYCE ROBINS

INCLUDING PHOTOGRAPHS BY
TIM WOODCOCK

CHANCELLOR
PRESS

ACKNOWLEDGEMENTS

The Publishers wish to thank the following individuals and organisations
for their kind permission to reproduce the photographs in this book:

All the photographs in this book have been supplied by **TIM WOODCOCK**
/TWP, except for the following:

JOHN BETHELL, St. Albans: 18, 29 top and 29 bottom, 114, 115, 114-5, 149 top, 152-3,
    162-3, 164-5, 170, 172-3, 189.
DOUGLAS CORRANCE: 170-1, 172, 178-9, 179, 180-1, 182-3, 184, 184-5, 185.
TREVOR DOLBY: 175.
ROBERT ESTALL PHOTO LIBRARY: 96 inset, 105, 148, 149 bottom, 154-5, 158 bottom.
HULTON PICTURE LIBRARY: 22.
LANDSCAPE ONLY: 12, 13, 20, 24-5, 66-7, 73, 80, 81, 84-5, 96-7, 100, 142, 150, 155, 161.
MARCUS LYON: 122-3, 130, 131 bottom, 158 top.
NATIONAL TRUST PHOTOGRAPHIC LIBRARY: 38-9, 41, 146-7, 156-7, 159, 160, 191,
    /JERRY HARPUR: 190, 191 bottom left.
OAKLEIGH PUBLICATIONS/D W H CLARK: 54 inset.
OCTOPUS PICTURE LIBRARY: 60 inset, 113 /BOB GIBBONS 30-1, 44-5, 117 top, 163;
    /JOHN FREEMAN: 132; /MICHAEL WARREN: jacket front, 40, 111.
OXFORD PICTURE LIBRARY/CHRISTOPHER ANDREWS: 22-3.
PHOTOBANK: 26-7, 101 /ADRIAN BAKER: 137, 202.
PITKIN PICTORIALS LTD.: 58-9.
ROBERT PEDERSEN: 8-9, 10 bottom, 17.
THE SLIDE FILE: 186-7, 188, 192, 194, 194-5, 196, 197, 198, 199, 200, 204, 205.
JUDY TODD: 203 bottom.
MARK WILLIAMS: Endpapers, 16, 72, 76-7, 79, 126-7, 128, 143.

EDITOR: ANNE CRANE   ART EDITOR: ROBIN WHITECROSS
PICTURE RESEARCHERS: EMILY HEDGES AND CHRISTINE RISTA
PRODUCTION: SIMON SHELMERDINE

First published in 1992 by Hamlyn, a division of Octopus Publishing Group
Published in 1997 by Chancellor Press

This 2002 edition published by Chancellor Press
an imprint of Bounty Books, a division of
Octopus Publishing Group, 2-4 Heron Quays, London E14 4JP

ISBN 0 7537 0536 2
Printed in China

CONTENTS

INTRODUCTION 7

THE THAMES VALLEY 8
HIGHWAY OF HISTORY

THE SOUTH AND SOUTH-EAST 26
ENGLAND'S GATEWAY

THE SOUTH-WEST 46
THE MAGIC & MYTH OF THE WEST COUNTRY

WALES 66
LAND OF THE RED DRAGON

THE MIDLANDS 86
ENGLAND'S HEARTLAND

EAST ANGLIA 106
THE BIG SKY COUNTRY

THE NORTH-EAST 126
MISSIONARIES, MARAUDERS, MOORS AND MILLS

THE NORTH-WEST 146
SUBLIME LAKES AND INDUSTRIAL STRENGTH

SCOTLAND 166
WILD CALEDONIA

IRELAND 186
LAND OF SAINTS AND SCHOLARS

INDEX 206

ABOVE: Sibsey Mill, Boston, Lincolnshire.
PAGE 2-3: Winceby, Lincolnshire Wolds.
PAGE 6-7: View from Woolland Hill looking west, North Dorset.

INTRODUCTION

The scenery of Britain and Ireland is always varied, often surprising and invariably fascinating, from the patchwork of tamed farmlands to the untouched wilderness of its deserted moors and craggy mountains. In England a single day's journey can take in gentle thatched villages around well-kept greens, mysterious windswept heaths and wave-nibbled cliffs. Though the geographical distance between the remote glens of Scotland, the hill farms of Wales and the flower-decked lanes of Ireland is small, each land has its own unique character. Throughout this beautiful country there are countless architectural gems, industrial monuments and strange legacies of prehistoric man to be discovered and explored by the traveller with time to spare.

HIGHWAY OF HISTORY

Once the great highway of London, the Thames flows past great abbeys, castles and mansions and there is no better way to view the grandeur of the capital, or the beauties of the river valley with its wooded hills, weirs and flower decked locks, than from a boat on its waters.

The view over the Thames from Richmond Hill is famous, and it has been much celebrated in the work of poets and artists. Sir Joshua Reynolds found the scene so beautiful that he had a house built on the hillside and from there painted a renowned summer landscape.

THE THAMES VALLEY

The Thames has played a vital role in Britain's history: without the river there would be no London. The Romans founded their city of Londinium at the first place they found suitable for building a bridge, and where their ships could supply them from Channel ports. Though at first Londinium covered only the original 'square mile' of the city, it quickly became Britain's major port and commercial centre, spreading and enlarging over the centuries, with the Thames the busiest and most important river in the country. The vital part it played in business life was underlined in the days when James I arrived from Scotland and demanded a huge loan from the City of London. When the mayor refused he threatened to remove his court and Parliament to Winchester and make a desert of Westminster. The Lord Mayor replied confidently that wherever the court went, the merchants of London would not be unduly worried because: 'Your Majesty cannot take the Thames with you.'

Today, many Thames-watchers lament the under-use of the river. The docks have lost much of their business with the introduction of containerization and the loss of trade towards the estuary, to Tilbury and beyond. Most of the great ships moored on the banks are now museums and though in 1820, when George IV came to the throne, 3,000 wherries were regularly plying for hire, today's pleasure cruisers seem like a small scattering by comparison. However, the waterway that was London's processional way for 1,000 years still comes into its own for major ceremonials, such as the funeral of Sir Winston Churchill, the river pageant for the Queen's Silver Jubilee and the opening of the Thames Barrier.

The great sweep of the river through the heart of London lays out the whole panorama of the capital, from the Palace of Westminster, past the Festival Hall, through the city, where Britain's tallest building, the National Westminster Bank headquarters, rises more than 183 m (600 ft), under Tower Bridge and into docklands, where the scene is changing faster than anywhere else in the capital. Here the old wharves are being turned into elegant shops, attractive restaurants and interesting galleries, canals are being renovated and basins are being turned into yacht harbours.

Though the importance of the Thames as a working river has declined, it has seen massive new developments over the past decade.

*The **THAMES BARRIER** (top), which lies between Greenwich and Woolwich, was completed in 1983 to protect London from the high tides that often caused serious damage and flooding. It is the largest movable flood barrier in the world, with 10 gates set in sills on the river bed, to be raised by hydraulic machinery when floods threaten.*

***CANARY WHARF** (above) is the most ambitious of the schemes to redevelop London's dockland. Standing on the site of the former West India Docks, on the Isle of Dogs, it includes offices, restaurants, shops, gardens and riverside promenades. Its most remarkable landmark is the 50 storey, 244 m (800 ft) tower in stainless steel.*

St Katharine's Dock, built in 1828, has now been turned into an up-market residential and commercial complex and houses the historic ships collection, with old sailing barges and Captain Scott's **Discovery**. London's maritime history is best expressed at Greenwich, with the famous square-rigged clipper **Cutty Sark**, the **Gipsy Moth IV**, in which Sir Francis Chichester sailed round the world single-handed in 1966, and as a climax, the Royal Naval College designed by Sir Christopher Wren and the superb 17th-century buildings of the National Maritime Museum.

In the early 19th century, many a fisherman made his living from the London stretch of the Thames, but pollution took its toll and by the middle of this century the waters were so dirty that no fish could survive there, and anyone who fell in needed a stomach pump. However, over the past 20 years, a great clean-up operation has purified the water so that 100 species of fish have returned. ▷ 15

*The **PALACE OF WESTMINSTER**, better known as the Houses of Parliament, is seen in full majesty from the south bank of the river (above). It occupies the site of a much older palace which was burned down in 1834. A competition held for a new design was won by architect Charles Barry, and it was built between 1840 and 1850, with Augustus Pugin providing all the elaborate ornamentation.*

***WESTMINSTER HALL**, part of the original palace saved from the fire, was built by William Rufus in 1097. It is 73 m (40 ft) long and has a magnificent hammerbeam roof added by Richard II in the 14th century.*

***BIG BEN**, the clock tower, houses a bell weighing 13½ tonnes, cast in a Whitechapel foundry in 1858 and named after Sir Benjamin Hall, the Commissioner of Works.*

The **TOWER OF LONDON** (above) has served, over the centuries, as palace, prison, execution site and home of the Royal Mint. The White Tower, the oldest part of the fortress, was designed for William the Conqueror by Gundulf, who also built Rochester Cathedral. The aim was to create a stronghold that would overawe the Londoners and from which any possible rebellion could be crushed. Henry III enlarged the tower and turned it into a mighty fortress.

ST JOHN'S CHAPEL, on the second floor of the White Tower, is the oldest church in London, where Henry IV created 46 knights in 1399. In the Chapel Royal of St Peter ad Vincula, rebuilt in 1307, are buried Anne Boleyn, Catherine Howard and Lady Jane Grey, who all lost their heads on **TOWER GREEN**, where a simple brass plate marks where the scaffold once stood.

ST PAUL'S CATHEDRAL (right) also has an eventful history. It is the fifth cathedral to stand on this site: one of its predecessors was vandalized by the Vikings and three succumbed to fire.

While the present cathedral was being built its architect, Sir Christopher Wren, lived in a house on the opposite bank of the Thames, so that he could watch every stage of the operation. The most prominent feature, the dome, is 111 m (365 ft) high and 357 m (122 ft) in diameter.

St Paul's has been the scene of many great public occasions, including the state funerals of Nelson, Wellington and Churchill and the wedding of Prince Charles and Lady Diana Spencer.

In London, the Thames is a tidal river but once past Teddington ('tide-ending-town') it changes its character. It becomes a sunny-faced pleasure river, where weekenders and holidaymakers cruise, punt and row past grand houses with carefully manicured lawns sweeping down to private moorings. On its way from its source near Cirencester it meanders through some of the most satisfyingly English countryside . The banks are still steeped in history: it flows past the broad water meadows of Runnymede, where King John was forced to sign the Magna Carta in 1215, and the dominating towers of Windsor Castle, where the river provides a natural moat, while across the water stands Eton College, founded in 1440 by Henry VI. At Cookham, cygnets are identified every July in an annual swan-upping ceremony, dating back to Elizabethan times. The artist Stanley Spencer lived here; his painting of the ceremony, with Cookham Bridge in the background,

*The **ALBERT MEMORIAL** (left) was designed in exuberant high-Victorian style by Sir George Gilbert Scott as a tribute to Prince Albert, consort to Queen Victoria, and was completed in 1876. The memorial was paid for by public subscription and the surplus went towards the building of the Albert Hall, on the other side of Kensington Gore. This vast amphitheatre is capable of holding 8000 people.*

*   **BROMPTON ORATORY** (above) is another elaborate late-Victorian edifice, opened in 1884, with the dome added 10 years later. The Italianate Roman Catholic church is heavily decorated with marble and statuary. Among the most interesting works are the apostle statues by Mazzuoli, dating from the 17th century.*

hangs in the Tate Gallery. At Henley-on-Thames, where it is spanned by a handsome 18th century five-arched bridge, the river straightens out sufficiently to form a regatta course. The world's first-ever regatta was held here in 1839 and became the Henley Royal Regatta under the patronage of Prince Albert in 1851. Its successor, held in July, is one of the high spots of the social calendar.

Pangbourne takes its name from a little trout stream called the Pang that flows into the Thames. Kenneth Grahame, author of **The Wind in the Willows** lived here and Mole and Ratty wandered this stretch of the river; readers try to guess which of the stately homes in the area was turned into Toad Hall. Jerome K. Jerome's hilarious heroes of **Three Men in a Boat**, required reading for all who venture out in river boats, stayed here at the Swan Inn. Above this pleasant Edwardian town, the Thames enters its only dramatic stretch, as it cuts through the Goring Gap in the south

As the river leaves central London and flows towards the lovely Thames valley, it passes the four distinctive chimneys of BATTERSEA POWER STATION (left). Designed by Sir Giles Scott, it opened in 1933 when it was announced as a 'temple of power'. It has been non-operational for some years and plans to turn it into an entertainment complex have been delayed by financial considerations.

Further up-river, at PUTNEY, keen oarsmen enliven the Thames scene (above). One of the most exciting river events of the year is the Oxford and Cambridge boat race, which has been rowed from Putney Bridge to Mortlake since 1845. The first bridge over the Thames at Putney was built in 1729 and was rebuilt by Bazalgette in 1886.

WINDSOR CASTLE (below), set in noble parkland, is the oldest British royal residence still in use and has been the home of kings and queens for 900 years. It has changed radically from the wooden fortress built on a chalk mound by William the Conqueror. In the 12th century Henry II built stone walls and towers, and the castle was extended by both Henry III and Edward III, though it was not until the 19th century, under George IV, with Sir Jeffry Wyatville as architect, that it was turned into a comfortable palace.

The State Apartments include a Rubens room and a Van Dyck room, and the dining room has a ceiling by Verrio and ornate wood carvings by Grinling Gibbons.

The grand medieval St George's Chapel contains the remains of many royal figures, including Henry VIII, Jane Seymour and Charles 1.

KEW GARDENS had its beginnings when Augusta, mother of George III, began collecting exotic foreign plants for the garden of her residence at Kew House, employing William Aiton as head gardener and the architect Sir William Chambers to decorate the grounds with classical and oriental buildings. George III combined these grounds with Richmond Lodge estate, and in 1841 the gardens were given to the nation. The Royal Botanic Gardens at Kew has an international reputation for its collections of plants and its work in distributing botanical information.

THE PALM HOUSE (right), one of Kew's most impressive sights, was inspired by Queen Victoria's visit to the conservatory built by Sir Joseph Paxton at Chatsworth. The great structure of glass and wrought iron was built in the 1840s to a design by Decimus Burton and covers 2,250 square

of the Chiltern Hills. The Chilterns are part of a chalk belt that stretches all the way from Yorkshire to Dorset, its valleys carved by rivers long since vanished, except for the Thames. Though often neglected by tourists interested only in 'sights', the Chilterns with their splendid woodlands make tempting walking and wandering country. From Coombe Hill, one of the highest points at 260 m (857 ft), there is a wide-ranging view across the Vale of Aylesbury and on the summit is a granite monument to the Buckinghamshire

metres (24,000 sq ft), housing a remarkable collection of palms from all over the world. Beside the Palm House, overlooking the pond, are replicas of the ten Queen's Beasts carved by James Woodford for the Coronation in 1953.

KEW PALACE (left), often known as the Dutch House, is one of the few remaining royal buildings in the area. It was built in 1631 by Samuel Fortrey, a prosperous London merchant, in the Flemish style popular at the time and leased to the Crown from 1727 onwards. George III retired here and his wife, Queen Charlotte, died here in 1818. The interior is still furnished as it was in their day and there is a collection of personal items belonging to George III and his family.

THE ORANGERY, designed for Princess Augusta in 1761 by Sir William Chambers, with windows on one side only, was both a greenhouse for orange trees and a place for the family to walk in poor weather.

men who perished in the Boer War. To the south-west lies Chequers, the Prime Minister's official residence, which has seen many toplevel meetings over the years.

Over the border in Oxfordshire stands the little town of Dorchester, where the Thames joins the river Thame. It has an impressive past, once an important Roman station, later a Saxon missionary centre and a famous cathedral city. St Birinus, who converted heathen Wessex from Dorchester, baptized the Saxon King Cynegils in the Thames in AD 635. Above Dorchester, where it flows through Oxford, the river is often called the Isis. This name probably came from a misinterpretation of the Roman name for the river, **Tamesis**. It was assumed that the name was a combination of Thames and Isis so that before the Thames joined the main river, it must be the Isis. The Thame is just one of the many tributaries that join the Thames along its course — the Cherwell, the Windrush and the Wey among them — running down from the uplands of Essex, Buckinghamshire, Berkshire, Northamptonshire, Gloucestershire and Surrey.　　□

The fine beech trees of the Chilterns (left) form a deep canopy that gives a cool and silent shade in summer. They are at their glorious best in autumn, when the leaves turn to russet and gold. The leaves are slow to rot and form a thick carpet beneath the trees. The beech — its name comes from the old English **bece** *— is a native tree.*

BURNHAM BEECHES, *part of an ancient forest that covered the Chilterns, is one of the world's largest collections of ancient beeches, many of which are over 300 years old.*

BISHAM *(above) is another scene of gentle, sylvan beauty, where the church stands so close to the river that it sometimes seems to be floating. The little Berkshire church has a remarkable collection of monuments to the Hoby family, especially the tomb of Elizabeth Hoby, with effigies of the whole family kneeling in prayer.*

The unique skyline of OXFORD (right)
caused Matthew Arnold to call it
'that sweet city with her dreaming spires'.
The university was established as early as
the 12th century by English students
expelled from the University of Paris.
University College was founded in the 13th
century, followed by Balliol and Merton.
The city has a wealth of handsome buildings
which have made it a popular tourist
centre, as well as a seat of learning.

The dome of the RADCLIFFE CAMERA
(centre) is a major landmark in the city's
centre. The first round library in the
country, it was built by James Gibbs and
completed in 1749. To the right is the spire
of ST MARY'S, and the cupola on the
SHELDONIAN THEATRE, the university's cere-
monial hall and Wren's first major work.

Alice's Adventures in Wonderland and *Through*
the Looking-Glass were inspired by the friendship
between Alice Liddell, daughter of the Dean
of Christ Church, and Charles Dodgson (above,
centre), a mathematics don. Dodgson loved
children and never tired of inventing stories for
Alice and her sisters as they wandered round
Oxford. He first wrote out the stories as a
Christmas present to 'a Dear Child in memory of a
Summer's day' in 1864, calling it *Alice's Adventures*
Under Ground. It was eventually published under its
new title and the name **LEWIS CARROLL**.

THE THAMES VALLEY

The *VALE OF THE WHITE HORSE,* in Oxfordshire (right), has a wealth of legends and ancient monuments. The white horse itself, a strange, stylized figure with spindly legs, is carved into the chalk, created to gallop for ever across the hillside. In past centuries it was credited with magical powers, and people believed it could grant wishes made by those standing in the horse's eye. The scouring, or cleaning, of the lines of the figure by local people used to be the occasion for a rowdy festival.

At the top of the hill is **UFFINGTON CASTLE,** an Iron Age fort commanding tremendous views over the surrounding countryside.

Below is the flat-topped **DRAGON HILL,** where St George is supposed to have killed the dragon. Legend says that the dragon's poisonous blood killed all the vegetation on the top, leaving the patch of bare chalk.

WAYLAND'S SMITHY, to the south-west, is a megalithic long barrow, said to be the home of an invisible blacksmith. Horses tethered nearby overnight, along with a coin for payment, were supposed to be newly shod by morning.

The origins of Britain's strange **LANDSCAPE SCULPTURES** are shrouded in mystery; no one knows when or why they were first carved. Some historians believe that the Uffington White Horse dates frcm the Iron Age, others think it was carved by Alfred to celebrate his victory over the Danes in 871. The Cerne giant, in Dorset, may be as much as 2000 years old, representing a Celtic god or possibly Hercules. The Westbury White Horse (left) is much more modern: it was cut on Bratton Down in Wiltshire in 1778 on the site of a an older figure.

ENGLAND'S GATEWAY

The traditional first sight of island Britain for travellers has always been the dazzling white cliffs of the south coast. For centuries unwelcome invaders landed on its beaches, bringing new cultures, but now the inviting coastal resorts, the ancient ports and the rural delights further inland tempt holidaymakers from home and abroad.

Julius Caesar beached his galleys in 55 BC on the shore at Deal, in Kent, after being repulsed at Dover. Before the coming of steamships, Deal was an important south coast port and a favourite haunt of smugglers. Offshore are the notorious Goodwin Sands, which have seen many shipwrecks over the years.

The shores of the south-east have always been the gateway to England, from the arrival of Julius Caesar in 55 BC to the opening of the Channel Tunnel in the 1990s. Richborough, near Deal, still has the foundations of the 24 m (80 ft) high triumphal arch built by the Emperor Claudius as his own 'gateway', together with the remains of one of the forts built to guard the Roman harbour. In 1066 came the Norman invaders, landing at Pevensey in East Sussex, an arrival depicted in the Bayeux tapestry, which shows sailors unloading the ships and leading the horses on to dry land. The town of Battle, which still retains much of its medieval character, grew up alongside the battlefield where William, Duke of Normandy, defeated the Saxon King Harold, who was felled by an arrow through the eye. The impressive remains of the Benedictine Abbey built by William still stands to commemorate his victory.

In the Middle Ages, when invasion from Europe was a constant threat, the fortified Cinque Ports – originally Hastings, Sandwich, Dover, Romney and Hythe – provided ships to serve the king for a number of days a year in return for special privileges, ▷ **32**

BODIAM CASTLE (above), in East Sussex, is the most romantic of medieval fortresses, its sturdy walls and towers reflected in the still moat, and it is often used as a film location. It was built by Sir Edward Dalyngrygge by licence of Richard II in 1385, to guard an important crossing of the river Rother against a possible invasion of the south of England from France. Its design is classic: a square of enclosing walls with a round tower at each corner, with square-cut gatehouses. It was 'slighted' by Cromwell's forces in the Civil War and remained uninhabited afterwards. Once in danger of being demolished, it was bought in the early 19th century by an eccentric MP known as 'Mad Jack Fuller'. It was then restored and given to the nation by Lord Curzon early this century. From the outside, it looks untouched.

The steep cobbled streets of **Rye**, East Sussex (above), have many lovely buildings dating from the 15th to 17th centuries, including the Mermaid Inn, which opened in 1420 and became the headquarters of a gang of smugglers. Small boats on the river (left) are a reminder of the past, before the harbour silted up, when Rye was one of the 'ancient towns' linked with the Cinque Ports and a target for raiders from the sea.

THE SOUTH AND SOUTH-EAST

THE SEVEN SISTERS, *the chalk cliffs east of Cuckmere Haven in East Sussex, are second only to the White Cliffs of Dover as the most famous landmarks of the south-east coast. The hills, with their springy downland turf, deep dips and steep summits, make challenging walking country and a severe testing ground for marathon runners.*

CUCKMERE HAVEN, *at the mouth of the meandering Cuckmere river, is an unspoilt bay, with a beach largely made up of fragments of chalk, together with flint nodules dissolved from the chalk (right). In the 19th century this lonely spot was the landing point for a brutal band of smugglers with their headquarters inland at Alfriston.*

THE SEVEN SISTERS COUNTRY PARK *covers 283 ha (700 acres) of downs, water meadows and undeveloped coastline. An interpretive centre is housed in a traditional 18th-century Sussex barn by the river and there is also a fascinating Living World Museum. Nature trails explore the area, where some 45 different species of plants have been identified.*

A short way inland is **WEST DEAN**, *a sleepy little village with high flint walls, a pond complete with ducks and a circular dovecote. Alfred the Great's palace is supposed to have stood on the site now marked by the ruins of a medieval manor.*

The South Downs Way runs along the top of the Seven Sisters to the great gash of **BIRLING GAP**, *where steep steps lead down to the sea, then on to the old Belle Tout lighthouse built in 1831.*

To the east is **BEACHY HEAD**, *standing 163 m (534 ft) above the sea, which was named 'Beau Chef' (beautiful head) by the Normans. From the top there are dramatic views and at the foot is a lighthouse which sends its beam 26 km (16 miles) out across the English Channel.*

and in the 13th century the fortified ports were strong enough to take on the whole French navy. Another major chapter in the history of England's defences came when Henry VIII rejected the authority of the Pope and courted the enmity of the countries of Catholic Europe. Reports of continental troops massing led to a flurry of defensive building: Dover Castle, which had guarded the shortest route across the Channel for four centuries, was strengthened and new fortifications were built all along the coast, including the castles of Deal and Walmer, Portland, Calshot and Hurst.

Henry VIII was a great collector of properties, among them some of the great houses of the south-east. He snatched Knole, near Sevenoaks, from Archbishop Cranmer, enlarging and enclosing the great deer park with its magnificent oaks and beeches, and he spent lavishly on improvements to the moated Leeds Castle. Where the King led, the aristocracy followed and, because of their proximity to London, the counties of Kent and Sussex have some of the finest houses in Britain. Loseley House was built with stone from

BRIGHTON'S PALACE PIER (below), its domes and pagodas echoing the extravagant Royal Pavilion, was opened in 1901, at the tail end of the enthusiastic pier-building phase of Victorian times. The older West Pier, built in 1863, has decayed over the years and was badly damaged by the 1987 hurricane, though there are still hopes of restoring it to its former glory. The most handsome of the town's piers, the graceful Chain Pier, built on the principle of suspension bridges in 1823, was smashed by a storm 73 years later.

Volk's Electric Railway runs from the Palace Pier to Black Rock. It was the first electric railway in Britain, pioneered by Magnus Volk and opened in 1883. The line follows Madeira Drive, which runs to the new Marina, the largest in Europe, covering 51 ha (126 acres), with moorings for more than 2,000 boats.

Waverley Abbey by a kinsman of Sir Thomas More; Sir John Baker, Queen Mary's Chancellor, built Sissinghurst Castle, later the home of Harold Nicolson and Vita Sackville-West. Petworth House was rebuilt by the 6th Duke of Somerset in the 17th century – later the grounds were landscaped by Capability Brown. And the 15th-century timber-framed manor house of Great Dixter was restored by Sir Edwin Lutyens.

The south coast resorts blossomed under the patronage of royalty. The Prince of Wales, later to become George IV, first visited Brighton in 1783 and was charmed by the town. He returned again and again, eventually renting a house in the Steyne, which over the years was transformed into the flamboyant Royal Pavilion. The aristocratic clique he gathered around him resulted in the building of the handsome Regency terraces which are among the town's most handsome features. When George V's physician advised Bognor as the

THE NEEDLES (above) are three chalk pinnacles projecting into the English Channel at the western tip of the Isle of Wight, with a small lighthouse standing on the furthest point. The power of the sea is constantly eating away at the chalk and changing its contours. The tallest of the stacks, a real 'needle' at 37 m (120 ft) collapsed in 1764 and an arch connecting the nearest stack to the mainland fell down in 1815. A lookout post on top of the sheer cliff gives good views, though the stacks look most impressive from the open sea.

ALUM BAY, nearby, is known for its muiti-coloured layers of sandstone, with 12 different shades, formed many milllons of years ago when the land was still under water.

best place for his convalescence, he assured the town of its prime position as a holiday resort, and its dignified title of Bognor Regis. Queen Victoria too, had an affection for the town, calling it her 'dear little Bognor'. However, the Victorian favourite was the Isle of Wight. Osborne House was built between 1845 and 1848 as a 'quiet and retired' home for her family, well away from public life.

Inland, the region has retained a surprisingly rural profile. Even Surrey, so much part of the commuter belt that it is nicknamed 'the Cockneys' backyard' has a gentle prettiness throughout its countryside. The green meadows of the Wey Valley still reach right into the heart of Guildford; the Hog's Back, running along a ridge between Guildford and Farnham, rivals any scenic drive in the south-east, and Hindhead stands high on the hillside amid woods and heathland with views out across Sussex and the Weald. Another exceptionally fine viewpoint is the 294 m (965 ft) high Leith Hill, with an 18th-century tower in the care of the National Trust. Hampshire is the third most densely wooded county in England, with yew and beech flourishing on the chalky soil and oak the traditional tree of the New Forest. The South Downs, their springy turf dotted with flowers, ▷38

SALEHURST (above), a pretty East Sussex village with a medieval church which it shares with nearby Robertsbridge, stands amid hopfields. The picturesque oast houses, with their pyramid roofs and white cowls, were built to dry hops, but in recent years many have been turned into homes.

Weatherboarding is characteristic of many houses in Kent, including the cottage at CHALK (left) where Charles Dickens and his bride spent their honeymoon. The forge, where Pip, in **Great Expectations,** *spent his boyhood, stands in the village.*

HOPS were first brought to England from Europe in the 16th century, when they were grown on small mounds, each with a group of poles. This method of cultivation can still be seen at the Museum of Kent Rural Life, near Maidstone. The more modern technique is to grow the hops up networks of strings supported by an overhead framework of wire. The hops send out their first small shoots in May and by late summer the frames are covered with abundant growth. Picking begins in late August when, in the past, thousands of pickers of all ages would flock in. Now machines have taken over, just as oil-fired sheds have taken over the drying work from the oast houses.

CANTERBURY CATHEDRAL (above) has been the mother church of Christendom in England since Saxon times. It was begun in 1070 by Archbishop Lanfranc, the first Norman archbishop, on the site of St Augustine's church.

It became a major pilgrimage centre after the canonization of Thomas à Becket in 1173. Becket's long and bitter feud with Henry II culminated in his murder by four of the King's knights in 1170. The pilgrims who flocked to his bejewelled tomb, eventually destroyed by Henry VIII in 1538, brought great prosperity to the city.

The choir dates from in the 13th century, the nave was reconstructed in the 15th century by Henry Yevele, who was responsible for the nave of Westminster Abbey. The central tower, 'Bell Harry', 72m (235 ft) high, was built in 1498.

The cathedral is renowned for its medieval stained glass, with scenes from the Old and New Testaments. The 12th-century South Window in Trinity Chapel has scenes from the life and death of St Thomas. The modern windows in the south-east transept are by the famous Hungarian artist Erwin Bossanyi.

The *NORMAN CRYPT* (right), the largest in Britain, is 70 m (230 ft) long and 40 m (130 ft) wide. Its Romanesque capitals are richly carved with a profusion of strange animals, grotesque heads and intricate patterns.

Fifty archbishops and one monarch, Henry IV, are buried within the cathedral, but the most remarkable tomb is that of Edward, the Black Prince, his brass effigy in full battle armour, near the site of St Thomas's original shrine.

curve across Sussex to end abruptly at the cliffs of Beachy Head, sheltering lonely farms and unspoilt villages. Kent, of course, is the 'garden of England' and its fertile soil and mild climate encouraged the Romans to plant orchards. Now Kent has half the total hectarage given to apple growing in England, three-quarters that of cherries and two-thirds pears.

'Kent sir', observed Mr Jingle in **Pickwick Papers**, 'Everybody knows Kent – apples, cherries, hops and women.' Pickwick's creator Charles Dickens knew Kent well; he spent his youth at Chatham and his last

years at Gad's Hill on the outskirts of Rochester and used the inns of Rochester and the town's Norman castle in **Pickwick Papers**. Several of his novels were written in Bleak House, above the harbour at Broadstairs, and the chief event in the town's calendar is the annual Dickens festival. The south-east has other notable literary associations. Chaucer's pilgrims trod the medieval track along a ridge of the North Downs to Canterbury still followed by walkers today; Jane Austen lived and wrote in her family's house at Chawton, in Hampshire, and is buried in Winchester Cathedral; Rudyard Kipling

38

POLESDEN LACEY, in Surrey, is a Regency mansion built and designed by Thomas Cubitt in the 1820s, on the site of an older house once owned by Richard Brinsley Sheridan, author of **The Rivals**.

In 1906 it was bought by the Hon. Ronald Greville and his wife Margaret, one of the leading society hostesses of her day. She entertained in luxurious style and Edward VII was among her eminent guests. Later, George VI and Queen Elizabeth spent their honeymoon at Polesden Lacey.

The house contains a great collection of china, Flemish and Mortlake tapestries and paintings including Dutch landscapes and 16th-century French court portraits. The sumptuous drawing room has gilded panelling from an Italian palace, lined with tall mirrors; even the ceiling shines with gold. When the room was re-gilded in the 1960s, it took more than 2,000 books of 24 carat gold leaf to complete the work.

found magic in the Sussex woods which 'know everything and tell nothing'. His 17th-century house Bateman's, at Burwash in East Sussex, is the house of **Puck of Pook's Hill** and the hill itself (Park's hill on modern maps) is along the valley.

The south is steeped in naval history. The Chatham dockyards were the birthplace of the great fighting ships upon which Britain's seapower depended, known as her 'wooden walls', from ships that sailed against the Spanish Armada to the fine warships of Trafalgar, **HMS Victory, Leviathan** and **Revenge. Victory**, launched in 1765, the flagship of Vice-Admiral Lord Nelson at the defeat of Napoleon's fleet, is on show at Portsmouth's Dockyard, and is still the flagship of the Commander-in-Chief, Naval Home Command. Here, too, are the Victorian battleship **HMS Warrior** and Henry VIII's flagship, the **Mary Rose**, raised in 1982 after lying on the bed of the Solent since 1545. This dockyard, home of the Royal Navy for 500 years, still fulfils a key role in the country's defences and is full of reminders of the days of Britain's greatness at sea.□

*The gardens of **SCOTNEY CASTLE** (left), near Lamberhurst in Kent, show the enormous care lavished on them by several generations of the Hussey family, who bequeathed them to the National Trust. The ruins of the 14th-century castle and a Tudor manor house nestle in a valley bright with rhododendrons and azaleas in early summer, though many of its lime trees were lost in the storms of 1987.*

***CHARTWELL** has its place among the historic properties of Kent because it was the home of Sir Winston Churchill for 40 years. The house contains many momentoes and personal possessions but the gardens (above) are among the chief delights. Churchill created the lake with its black swans, planted the orchard trees and built the wall round the kitchen garden. The Golden Rose Garden was planted to mark the Churchills' golden wedding in 1958.*

Nymans (below) is a fascinating National Trust garden in West Sussex, begun by Ludwig Messel in 1885. It consists of a series of small, intimate gardens packed with good things: old-fashioned roses, heathers and wide herbaceous borders with an informal profusion of flowers, and a huge collection of rhododendrons, magnolias and camellias, among them hybrids named after members of the family. The walled garden has an Italian stone fountain as its centre-piece, guarded by four large topiary pieces. One of the delights of the gardens is the lack of over-planning. Fruit trees flourish among spring flowers, just as they would in an informal cottage garden. Part of the great house was burned down in 1947 and its empty shell forms a romantic backdrop for lawns and flowers.

CISSBURY RING (above) is a distinctive hill-fort high on the South Downs to the east of Findon, its double ramparts enclosing 30 ha (74 acres).

Named after a Saxon chieftain, Cissa, it was occupied from around 300 BC and was re-fortified towards the end of the Roman period. A Romano-British shrine and pottery dating from the 1st to the 3rd century AD have been uncovered.

Hundreds of years before Cissbury became a fortress, Neolithic man mined flint here and the hollows and mounds on the surface are evidence of the many shafts sunk below. A wide variety of primitive tools have been discovered and identified.

MARK ASH (left) is the largest of the New Forest beechwoods, with many huge and ancient trees. Called the 'Ancient and Ornamental' woods, they are so thickly canopied by branches and foliage that no undergrowth or flowers grow on the mossy carpet. Oak is the traditional tree of the forest and there are several fine specimens, chief among them the Knighthood Oak, some 600 years old, with a girth measuring 7 m (22 ft) at 1 m (4 ft) from the ground.

In 1079 William the Conqueror proclaimed the New Forest a royal hunting ground, administered under a strict code of forest law. Today the area is under the care of the Forestry Commission and the laws are administered by a Court of Verderers, who meet in the 17th-century Queen's House at **LYNDHURST**, the busy 'capital' of the Forest.

As well as the extensive woodlands for which it was named, the New Forest contains flowery pasture, moor and heath-land, bogs and glades high in bracken. Large numbers of sturdy little ponies roam freely, though they all belong to those with 'commoner' grazing rights and are regularly rounded up for branding and selling. Deer are also plentiful, most of them fallow deer, descended from the animals hunted by William the Conqueror. Red deer and the roe deer can be difficult to spot.

Within the bounds of the forest are a number of delightful villages, such as old-world **MINSTEAD**, with its 13th-century church looking like a row of cottages, with tiers of galleries and a family pew complete with its own fireplace. **CADNAM** has an inviting thatched inn and **ROCKBOURNE**'s single street is set along a winding stream and lined with Tudor and Georgian houses, alternating with thatched cottages.

THE MAGIC & MYTH
OF THE WEST COUNTRY

*The echoes of distant times
fill the gentle hills, the
wild moorlands and the rugged
shoreline of the west of
England. From the standing
stones of Cornwall and
the Iron Age settlements of
Dorset to the haunts of
the great seafarers of glorious
battles, reminders of past
centuries are ever-present.*

*Eggardon Hill stands 244 m (800 ft) above the
Vale of Marshwood in Dorset, with commanding views
across rolling countryside to the sea. Its Iron Age
hill-fort, with three vast ramparts rising 9 m (30 ft), is
the most impressive of a series of forts constructed
along the chalk hillside, cared for by the National Trust.*

Mystery, myth and legend seem inextricably bound up with the landscape of the West Country. From olden times come the legends of King Arthur, who held court at Camelot and was buried on the Isle of Avalon, and fearsome tales of ghostly beasts that roam the moors at night. Far more recent are the stories of smugglers, landing their contraband in deserted coves, and wreckers, plundering ships unfortunate enough to run aground on the savage coast and unwilling to leave survivors as witnesses.

Ancient civilizations have left their puzzles behind, chief among them the great stone circles. The most famous, Stonehenge, still preserves its mysteries in spite of endless attempts by the experts to explain its purpose. Even less is known about the far larger circle at nearby Avebury, where the stones are unhewn; some are tall and upright, others short and dumpy, possibly representing male and female figures. Comparatively

STOURHEAD, the great Palladian mansion built in the 18th century for the Hoare family in Wiltshire, has gardens created as the picture of an ideal Italian landscape by Henry Hoare II. The centrepiece is the lake (below) reflecting trees and flowers, crossed by an ornamental five-arched bridge. The garden wall unfolds a series of views: the Temple of Apollo, the woodland grotto, the Temple of Flora, seen across the water.

*OARE WATER VALLEY, a wooded Exmoor coombe (right), has links with the romantic tale of **Lorna Doone**. Novelist R. D. Blackmore used the little square-towered church at Oare for the most dramatic scene in the story, where Lorna, about to be married to John Ridd, is shot through the window by the outlaw Carver Doone.*

CULBONE CHURCH, nestling in a deep glade in a hidden corner of Somerset, which can only be reached on foot, is the smallest English church still used regularly, measuring only 10 m (34 ft) long and 4 m (12ft 4 ins) wide. The building is mainly Norman, with a small slated steeple, and its oldest feature is a little square window in the chancel, cut from a single block of stone. In medieval times a colony of lepers lived in the woods nearby and took the sacraments through a side window.

few visitors find the 'Merry Maidens' near St Buryan in Cornwall, said to be 19 girls who were turned to stone by the devil for dancing when they should have been praying. Many people still believe that the standing stones have magical properties and some modern investigators are convinced that all the sites are linked by lines of force that carry powerful psychic energy.

The West Country has great tracts of land almost untouched by modern development – the wildernesses of Dartmoor, Exmoor and Bodmin, the vast chalk expanse of Salisbury Plain – where the relics of primitive man have been able to remain undisturbed. Evidence of the earliest settlements have been found deep within the ground, with the discovery of 12,000-year-old skeletons in the Cheddar caves, and the round stone huts of Iron Age farmers which litter the peaks of Bodmin Moor. Dartmoor has more than 2,000 hut circles. The earthworks of Maiden Castle in Dorset are the most impressive of their kind and the ancient village of Chysauster has well-preserved Bronze Age houses in a style unique to the Lizard Peninsula.

The beauty and elemental grandeur of the West Country has influenced many well-known writers, their books seeming to have grown out of the landscape. The brooding quality of the 'untamed' heathland of mid-Dorset, softened now as a result of planting by the Forestry Commission, pervades the novels of Thomas Hardy. Daphne du Maurier uses the coast and the countryside of Cornwall to great effect. Her Jamaica Inn,

BATH, famous as a spa since Roman times, owes its elegant Georgian architecture to its fashionable heyday in the 18th century, when it was the favourite gathering place for Beau Nash and his aristocratic circle. The sweeping semicircle of Royal Crescent (below left) was designed by John Wood the Younger. His father was responsible for the equally famous Queen Square and the Circus. The honey-coloured stone for the buildings came from quarries owned by one of their patrons, Ralph Allen.

WELLS CATHEDRAL, *built between the 12th and 14th centuries, is one of Somerset's most beautiful buildings. Among the many fascinating features are the great, branching stone staircase (left) that leads to the Chapter House with its fan-vaulted ceiling, the 14th-century astronomical clock where knights emerge to joust every hour, and the lovely Lady Chapel. Originally, 400 statues graced the west front; many have been lost but it still makes an imposing spectacle.*

The **TITHE BARN** *at Bradford-on-Avon in Wiltshire was built by the Abbess of Shaftesbury, somewhere around the time that Wells Cathedral was completed. The enormous arched timbers of the roof cover a granary 51 m (168 ft) long (above). Bradford has long been a prosperous little town, thus accumulating some interesting buildings over the centuries, including a Saxon church and the mansions of well-to-do wool merchants from the 16th and 17th centuries.*

isolated on the forbidding Bodmin Moor, became so famous that it is now the haunt of tourists, rather than smugglers, but Frenchman's Creek, near Helston, still has an air of quiet mystery. The band of outlaws who terrorized the vlllages of Exmoor in the 17th century were immortalized in R.D. Blackmore's **Lorna Doone**.

Many of the legends of this part of Britain are as fascinating as the landscape. Dozmary Pool, dark and silent on Bodmin Moor, is said to be bottomless, and the sighing wind is the lament of a wicked lord named Tregeagle, condemned for ever to empty the pool with a holed limpet shell. Dozmary is also reputed to be the spot where a hand rose from the water to receive King Arthur's sword Excalibur. Arthur is supposed to have lived at Tintagel, where the shell of a medieval castle perches precariously on dramatic cliffs, and to have died on Glastonbury Tor, site of the 'fairy isle' of Avalon. It was on the Tor, according to legend, that Joseph of Arimathea buried the Holy Grail and on nearby Wearyall Hill his staff took root as a thorn tree, a cutting of which still grows in the abbey grounds. ▷ 57

SOMERSET is a county of peace and charm, its Old English name meaning the land of the 'summer-farm dwellers'. Apart from its cider and cheese, it is known for its pretty villages, interesting towns and lovely old houses.

*CREWKERNE (left) dates back to Anglo-Saxon times when it minted its own coins, and was later famous for its sailcloth, providing the sails for Nelson's **Victory** and for America's Cup competitors. The 15th-century church, made from the golden local limestone, has an imposing west front and fine stained glass. A recess in the wall may once have been a hermit's cell.*

BRYMPTON D'EVERCY (above) is a Norman manor house with 16th and 17th century additions, which claims the longest straight staircase in England. The buildings, in warm Ham stone, are attractively grouped round a courtyard.

The **DORSET COAST**, running east
from Weymouth, is a magnificent
sweep of chalk cliffs, crowned by emerald
turf and backing wide sandy bays.
The most beautiful stretch begins beyond
the 152 m (500 ft) cliff of White Nothe,
with Man o' War Bay and St Oswald's Bay
and the limestone outcrops which
first show themselves as reefs, the Cow and
Calf Rocks and the Blind Cow, then
as a headland in which the sea has carved
the famous arch of **DURDLE DOOR**,
12 m (40 ft) high.

At Dungy Head the limestone cliffs begin
but at **LULWORTH COVE** the sea has
broken through the outer layer and carved
out the bay from the soft chalk behind,
leaving it sheltered by two limestone arms.
On the eastern slope is a forest of
fossilized tree stumps, hollowed out over the
centuries; to the west is the Cathedral
Cavern where pillars of rock support the
vault of the roof and the Stair Hole, another
'door' in the making. At Worbarrow
Bay, 3 km (2 miles) further along the coast,
there is a pyramid of stratified rock that
is a geologist's delight.

At **EAST LULWORTH** are the ruins
of Lulworth Castle, dating from the 16th
and 17th centuries but largely destroyed by
fire in 1929. Its chapel, known as the
Rotunda, was the first Roman Catholic
church built with official permission after
the Reformation.

The **LULWORTH SKIPPER**, a small golden
brown and black butterfly with a 25-27 mm (approx
1 in) wingspan, was first discovered and recorded at
Durdle Door in 1832. Large colonies are found in
the coarse grass of the hillsides and clifftops of
southwest Dorset between Weymouth and Swanage
in July and August. The butterfly, which can be
identified by a golden 'peacock eye' on the upper
forewing, is extremely rare outside this area.

The West Country can offer wild uplands, sheltered picture postcard villages, magnificent cathedrals and picturesque little churches, but its crowning glory is its coastline. Dorset, besides the inviting sandy beaches of resorts like Weymouth, favoured by George III, and Bournemouth, beloved of the Victorians, has the amazing Chesil Bank, a 29 km (18 miles) long wall of shingle, rising as high as 14 m (45 ft), where gem-hunters can find coloured jaspers and quartz – and sometimes treasure from Spanish galleons. In Devon the north coast, with stark cliffs, dramatic valleys and roads that plunge suddenly seawards, contrasts with the sandy coves, palm trees and subtropical flowers of the south. Cornwall has 241 km (150 miles) of coast, with wild headlands and secret caves and moods of great savagery, when angry waves crash onto unyielding rocks. The remains of many ships lie offshore and the churchyards have received numerous sailors through the centuries.

The maritime traditions are strong and enduring, and Devon is proud of the important role its seamen played

DEVON's two coastlines offer resorts of widely differing character.

CLOVELLY was a quiet fishing village until the mid-19th century, when Charles Dickens and Charles Kingsley both wrote about it and brought the first of the tourists; now it is one of north Devon's showplaces. Its steep cobbled street (left) zigzags down to the harbour, past pretty old cottages decked with fuchsias and roses. Cars are not allowed and donkeys are still used to carry goods and luggage.

EXMOUTH has been one of south Devon's most popular holiday resorts since the early 18th century, known for its sandy beaches and safe bathing. It stands at the mouth of the River Exe estuary (above), where the sea sweeps in round Straight Point, piling up sand on the shore, leaving only a slim channel for vessels.

THE SOUTH-WEST

in the history of the Elizabethan age, when the Spanish Armada threatened Britain's shores. Sir Francis Drake was born in the market town of Tavistock, on the edge of Dartmoor's wilderness, but made his home in Plymouth where he became mayor. It was here that he returned after becoming the first Englishman to circumnavigate the world.

His statue gazes out to sea from the famous Hoe, where he insisted on finishing his game of bowls before dealing with the Armada, and which still commands one of the finest harbour views in the country. Sir Walter Raleigh was born in the 16th-century farmhouse of Hayes Barton, and his father was churchwarden at the church of East Budleigh, a typically pretty Devon village of cob and thatched cottages. Bideford with its handsome 15th-century bridge and tree-lined quay, was once a major port and its seamen were famed throughout the world. The best known was Sir Richard Grenville, who obtained the town's charter from Elizabeth I, and history remembers him best for the heroic but ill-fated stand of his ship, the *Revenge*, and its Bideford crew against 15 Spanish ships in the Azores.

Dartmouth, beautifully situated on a hillside above the lovely river Dart, was England's greatest port in the Middle Ages, and it was here that the ships of the Second and Third Crusades assembled before setting out for the Holy Land. It is dominated by the Royal Naval College and fishing still flourishes here, though much of the town's revenue now comes from tourism. Many of the West Country ports share the same story. When the pilchard industry was at its height, the Cornish harbours of St Ives and Mousehole were centres of a prosperous trade. Once the cellars of the fishermen's cottages were used to salt and store pilchards, and the narrow streets were filled with the smell of fish. Now many of the granite and slate cottages have been converted into shops, restaurants and art studios and in summer the streets are thronged with holidaymakers.

WILTSHIRE is a county with its roots deep in the past and it has some of the most remarkable legacies of prehistoric man in Britain.

STONEHENGE may have been built as an open temple for sun worship or an astronomical observatory; in either case it was a stupendous feat of megalithic engineering which began 5,000 years ago. Gigantic sarsen stones, weighing up to 50 tonnes, were dragged here from the Marlborough Downs 30 km (20 miles) away, in the days before wheeled vehicles.

On CHERHILL DOWN (above), the Iron Age fort of Oldbury Castle overlooks an area rich in ancient barrows and enclosures. Nearby is the 19th-century Lansdowne Column, 38 m (125 ft) high, erected by the 3rd Marquis of Lansdowne to honour a distinguished ancestor, Sir William Petty.

THE SOUTH-WEST

DARTMOOR's untamed wilderness stretches across south-west Devon, splendid in its desolation. Granite tors, the remnants of a three million-year-old mountain system, dot the hillsides.

At **HOUND TOR** (right), a devil dog is said to haunt the moor, hunting out unbaptized children, and this legend inspired Sir Arthur Conan Doyle's **The Hound of the Baskervilles**. Near the Tor are the remains of a medieval village, its buildings dating from the 12th and 13th centuries, excavated in 1961.

WISTMAN'S WOOD (below) is one of the moor's strangest areas, where clumps of stunted oaks, some over 600 years old, grow among inhospitable boulders. The dwarf trees, standing 396-427 m (1,300-1,400 ft) above sea level, well above the normal level for trees on the moor, never grow more than a few metres high and moss and ivy cover their gnarled limbs.

THE HURLERS (below), three stone circles on the wilds of Bodmin Moor, are just one of the reminders that prehistoric man lived on the bleak slopes left uninhabited in modern times. The stones are all much the same height but the three circles measure 41 m (135 ft), 34 m (110 ft) and 32 m (105 ft) respectively. Legend says that they were once men, turned to stone as a punishment for playing the ancient game of hurling on the Sabbath. A few kilometres away is Trevethy Quoit, a 4,000-year-old chambered tomb, and on the north side of the moor is an enclosure known as King Arthur's Hall, probably built at roughly the same time to protect livestock.

A single road crosses the moor with its great peaks of Brown Willy and Rough Tor, both over 400 m (1,312 ft), the highest points in Cornwall.

COTEHELE HOUSE (above), standing in the sheltered Tamar Valley, a complete contrast to the stark Bodmin landscape, has scarcely changed since it was built in early Tudor times. A romantic grey stone house built around two courts, it still has the original furniture and tapestries collected by the Edgecumbe family. The great hall is 12 m (40 ft) long, with an open timbered roof and rough stone floor, but in spite of the grandeur of the main rooms the house still retains the atmosphere of a family home. In the Jacobean tower is a magnificently carved drawing-room door with a pattern of roses, and a bedroom where Charles I spent the night. The manorial water mill is still in working order and the quay, on the banks of the river, has 200-year-old boathouses.

THE SOUTH-WEST

TRESCO *is the second largest of the 'hundred isles of Scilly', 45 km (28 miles) off the westernmost tip of England's mainland at Land's End. Once, some 4,000 years ago, Scilly was a single island, but the power of the sea has divided it into fragments, leaving five inhabited islands, many islets that are home to seabirds, seals and puffins, and scores of barren rocks. Legend says that the islands are the remains of the lost land of Lyonesse, once joined to Cornwall but flooded by Merlin to drown the enemies of the slaughtered King Arthur, who were pursuing the last of his followers.*

CROMWELL'S CASTLE (left), Scilly's best-known monument, is in an excellent state of preservation, though the promontory on which it stands had to be reinforced with granite to prevent it from being cut off from the rest of the island. Though Cromwell himself never came here, the round gun-tower was built in 1651, after the Roundhead assault on Scilly. It guards the channel between Tresco and Bryher, the smallest of the inhabited islands, where the few residents live by fishing and farming.

Though the northern end of Tresco, where the castle stands, is wild and rugged, further south are the famous Abbey Gardens, laid out by Augustus Smith in 1834, using plants obtained from the Royal Botanic Gardens at Kew. Pines and cypresses protect luxuriant plants from many countries, including New Zealand, South Africa, Australia, Japan and China. The sunny dry summers and mild winters of Scilly mean that subtropical flowers and plants flourish throughout the islands. Flowers are vitally important to the economy and are exported in bud from December onwards. From February onwards, wild and cultivated flowers abound.

LAND OF THE RED DRAGON

The glory of Wales, the proud land of princes, is the savage grandeur of its mountains, as well as the softer beauty of its sheep-dotted hills, fertile green valleys and tumbling rivers. Seekers of gentle solitude will always be refreshed by the timeless beauty of the Welsh countryside.

The small hill farms of the Black Mountains consist mainly of rough grazing, with farmers keeping flocks of breeding ewes. The favourite breed of sheep is the hardy Welsh Mountain, well-adapted to the severe weather of the uplands. In late spring, the ewes are brought down to the farms for lambing.

The word 'Welsh' derives from the Anglo-Saxon word for 'foreigners', a reminder that this principality of Wales has always preserved its own separate identity, language and national aspirations. In the 8th century the powerful King Offa of Mercia built the dyke that bears his name, a massive earthwork which ran from Prestatyn on the River Dee in the north of the country to the Severn estuary near Chepstow in the south. Historians have long debated the purpose of the dyke, which seems a gigantic undertaking for a simple boundary marker, yet would hardly have served as an adequate military defence. Whatever the original intention, it was remarkably effective, not only keeping the Celts out of England, but also keeping the English out of Wales. The earth barrier probably played an important role in preserving the feeling that Wales is a separate land, even without the presence of physical barriers or tangible borders. ▷ 72

The ruins of two ancient monastic foundations in Gwent rival one another in the beauty of their setting. LLANTHONY PRIORY (above) stands in the lonely and beautiful Vale of Ewyas, the peaceful site chosen by Hugh de Lacy, Earl of Hereford, who founded the priory in 1108. He prayed that it might never be spoiled by growing rich, but by the end of the century corruption had set in.

TINTERN ABBEY (right) is set in lush green meadows beside the River Wye – its beauty inspired William Wordsworth to write a poem in its praise. The Cistercian Abbey was founded in 1131 and along with the great roofless church a number of monastic buildings still stand, including the Chapter House, refectory and kitchen.

WALES

The **Usk Valley** *is a place of pastoral peace with low hills and quiet villages, remaining virtually untouched by modern development. The river rises in the Black Mountains and follows the boundary between Dyfed and Powys through rich farmland, always staying within sight of the mountains, until it joins the Severn estuary at Newport.*

On its journey it flows beneath the 13-arched bridge at **Crickhowell**, *dating originally from the 16th century, and the six high arches of the 18th-century bridge at* **Llangynidr**. *It also feeds a reservoir near Llandovery, created to supply Swansea with water, which is surrounded by dark conifers planted by the Forestry Commission.*

The town of **Usk** *was called Burrium by the Romans, for whom it was an important station. The castle was originally built in the 12th century as one of the strongholds of the Marcher lords and was left in ruins after its owners supported the Royalist cause in the Civil War.*

Abergavenny *is a riverside market town guarded by mountains with splendid viewpoints: the Skirrid to the east, the Sugar Loaf to the north and the Blorenge to the south-east. The remnants of the Norman castle founded in the 11th century stand in a pleasant park. In the following century it was in the hands of William de Braose, notorious in Welsh history for his massacre of the local chieftains after inviting them to Christmas dinner. Adjoining the ruins is a museum of local history, including costumes and craft tools.*

After the Norman Conquest, William set up powerful barons along the borders of his kingdom, in order to keep the troublesome Welsh princes in check. These Marcher Lords built castles like Chepstow, Grosmont and Skenfrith and encroached further and further on to Welsh land through a series of skirmishes. In the early days, when Wales was divided by warring factions, they met little effective opposition, but with the rise of a new breed of Welsh princes, the Llywelyns, a serious clash was inevitable. After a major battle resulting in the defeat of Llywelyn II, Edward I built a chain of great fortresses, the magnificent castles of Conwy, Harlech, Beaumaris and Caernarfon among others, to safeguard against future rebellion. To salve Welsh pride, Edward promised them a Prince of Wales 'unable to speak English' and presented his baby son, born at Caernarfon in 1301. The tradition has survived to modern times, with the investiture of Prince Charles in 1969.

Though Wales has been united with England since Henry VIII passed the Act of Union in 1535, by which English became the official language of law and government, the Welsh people have a strong sense of

*The countryside of Wales contains many contrasts: sometimes gently rural, with old barns (above) looking over lush fields, sometimes dramatic, as in the **BRECON BEACONS NATIONAL PARK** (right), with its magnificent mountains and red sandstone peaks. Its backbone is the 'great escarpment' extending nearly 65 km (40 miles) from east to west.*

*The Beacons are so called because the hilltops were used for signal fires in the days before telecommunications, and the highest point is **PEN-Y-FAN** at 886 m (2,906 ft). The Beacons are popular with walkers but they can be hazardous, with sheer precipices dropping hundreds of metres.*

*The belt of limestone in the south of the park contains a complete and extensive system of caves and underground passages. The **DAN-YR-OGOF** caves, with their strange stalagmite and stalactite formations and underground lakes in huge caverns, are a popular tourist attraction.*

tradition and their language survived to achieve official status once more. Road signs are in Welsh as well as English and a Welsh television channel acts as a boost to Welsh drama and poetry. At least one in four Welsh people speak the language, including some thousands in rural areas who speak only Welsh, and the number of bi-lingual schools is increasing.

The most highly populated part of the country is the south, especially around the capital city of Cardiff, where docks and factories provide employment. In the valleys, so long synonymous with coal mining, the rivers still run black, but chimneys no longer belch smoke and the slopes are green. The scenery may have gained but the tightly-knit mining communities have lost, with many younger people forced to move away in search of work. All the same, this is still the place of brass bands and superb male voice choirs. Many of the great pits are now part of history. At the Big Pit, Blaenavon, closed in 1980, visitors can experience a

CAERPHILLY CASTLE (right), in Mid Glamorgan, is the largest of Welsh castles, a great medieval fortress built by Gilbert de Clare in 1268 on the site of a Roman fort. Its land and water defences were formidable, with massive walls, towers and moats which made it impossible for attackers to use most of the tactics of siege warfare. The outstanding feature inside the castle is the Great Hall, designed in grand style in the 14th century and lovingly restored.

West Glamorgan boasts the lovely 29 km (18 mile) Gower Peninsula, its westernmost point WORMS HEAD, winding out into the sea like a snake (below), guarding the 5 km (3 mile) arc of sand of Rhosili Bay. The nearby coastline has seen many a shipwreck, and the gaunt ribs of one vessel still appear above the water at low tide.

little of the everyday working environment of miners, and a disappearing way of life is captured in the Afon Argoed Country Park near Swansea.

Only part of south Wales is industrialized; there are also many unscathed areas of outstanding natural beauty. The Pembroke coast is a National Park, with a 273 km (170 mile) path running from St Dogmaels, near Cardigan, to Amroth beyond Saundersfoot Bay along cliffs which are bright with wild flowers and busy with seabirds. The wild charm of the Gower Peninsula culminates in the headland and dunes at Rhosili. The northern coast of Gower is fringed by marshlands and saltings, with the mudflats of Penclawdd supporting millions of cockles. The Brecon Beacons, offering wide panoramas of mountain and moorland, sweep right down to the very doorstep of the south Wales coalfields.

The coast of north Wales is the favoured holiday destination of Midlanders and the string of resorts including Rhyl, Prestatyn and Colwyn Bay has been heavily anglicized by the yearly influx, peppered with amusements, while the aroma of fish and chips and candy floss mixes with the tang of salt in the air. The mood changes perceptibly in Llandudno, with its elegant Victorian houses and the great crescent of sand nestling between two headlands, the Great Orme and Little Orme. The isle of Anglesey, often overlooked in favour of the more spectacular mountain country of the mainland, has 160 km (100 miles) of varied coastline, remains of civilizations dating back 4,000 years, and a large proportion of Welsh speaking inhabitants.

WALES

Snowdonia National Park, with its vast expanses of craggy mountains, glacier-carved valleys, turbulent streams and forest-sheltered lakes, is a mecca for walkers and climbers. Amid the wild grandeur of the mountains, it is easy to believe the legends of a fearsome giant who wore a cloak woven from the beards of the men he had killed, and who was finally slain by King Arthur and buried on the summit of Snowdon, Yr Wyddfa Fawr ('the tomb'). Even more hateful was the monster, Afanc, supposed to lie beneath the waters of the 'green lake', Glaslyn. Afanc terrorized the Vale of Conwy for years until the local people eventually schemed to bind him with chains, then they dragged him up the mountain and hurled him into the lake.

ST GOVAN'S CHAPEL (left) is a tiny building wedged deep in a cleft of the cliffs near Bosherton in Dyfed. The building itself is 13th century, but is built on the site of a much older hermit's cell, though the identity of St Govan is shrouded in mystery: one story is that he was Sir Gawain, one of the knights of King Arthur, another says that he was a 5th-century Irish saint.

Further along the cliffs is the Elegug Stack, a lofty column of limestone crowded with seabirds in the breeding season.

To the west, the heather-clad Lleyn Peninsula reaches out like a long finger into the Irish Sea. It is a peaceful, unhurried region which preserves the remnants of ancient cultures: there are neolithic tombs, Iron Age hill-forts and the scores of hut circles of Tre'r Ceiri, the 'town of giants'. Off the tip of the peninsula lies Bardsey Island, where Welsh monks took refuge when the marauding Saxons destroyed their monasteries. It was known as the 'Island of 20,000 Saints', because of the number of holy men said to be buried there, and it was once an important pilgrimage site: two pilgrimages to Bardsey were said to equal one pilgrimage to Rome. ▷ 80

In the ELAN VALLEY, POWYS, a series of dams and reservoirs (above) were constructed in the late 19th and early 20th centuries to contain the waters of the River Elan as a water supply for Birmingham. The houses, farms and church of the valley now lie beneath the water, including the house in which the poet Shelley lived and wrote between 1811-12.

The result is some of the most popular lake scenery of Wales; when the water level is high, the water cascades over the great dams.

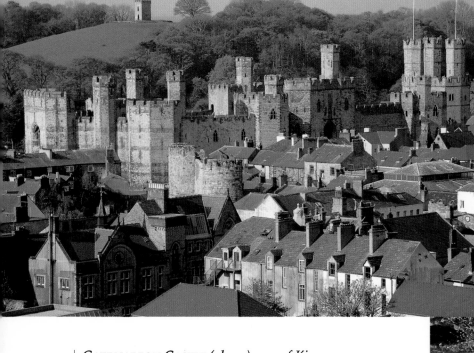

CAERNARFON CASTLE (above), one of King Edward I's fortresses, was designed as the seat of government, demonstrating the king's power over the Welsh. It stands majestically on the Menai Strait in Gwynedd, the scene of two royal investitures: Prince Edward in 1911 and Prince Charles in 1969. The castle has seen several reverses of fortune: it was captured and sacked by the Welsh in 1294, fought off Owain Glyndwr in the 15th century and was finally captured by the parliamentarians in the Civil War.

The valley of the RIVER ARTRO (right), further south in Gwynedd, has a much longer history than the castle at Caernarfon, and its scattering of prehistoric sites suggests that it was once an area of special religious significance. The village of LLANBEDR, on the Artro estuary, has Bronze Age cairns and ancient standing stones. Nearby are the so-called Roman Steps, an impressive stone stairway up the mountain, probably laid out as a medieval packway from one valley to the next.

WELSH RIVERS are popular with anglers and most contain plentiful brown trout. Some are known for sea trout, which grow large feeding in the rich waters of the Atlantic Ocean, before finding their way upstream. Their numbers have increased in recent years, while the numbers of salmon coming into the fresh water to spawn has decreased because of over-fishing in the ocean.

WALES

The Prime Minister David Lloyd George was brought up on the Lleyn Peninsula, at Llanystumdwy (the 'church at the bend of the river'), where there is a museum to his memory. The grave of the 'Welsh wizard' is encased in local stone and covered by a boulder, his favourite spot for sitting and meditating beside his beloved stream. T.E. Lawrence is another of the famous sons of Wales, born at Tremadog on the Lleyn Peninsula. A monument to ex-miner and politician Aneurin Bevan, the architect of Britain's National Health Service, stands on a hillside near his home town of Tredegar in the valleys. The current leader of the Labour Party, Neil Kinnock, was born in the same area.

Wales has probably produced more great figures in the field of the arts than any other nation, taken as a percentage of the population. Actor Richard Burton came from Pontrhydyfen, near Port Talbot; the pretty coastal resort of Tenby was the birthplace of Augustus John, and displays a number of his paintings in the local museum; the poet Dylan Thomas lived and worked at Laugharne, supposed to be the Llareggub of **Under Milk Wood**, where his boat shed study is now a museum. Every year at the National Eisteddfod, the Bardic chair and crown is still awarded for Welsh poetry and the festival embraces solo and choral singing, recitation and the playing of musical instruments. □

*BLAENAU FFESTINIOG (left) is a town of
slate: blue-grey slate that provides its
roofing, paving and fencing, even its tomb-
stones. In the last century slate was a
booming industry and the north Wales
quarries supplied roofing for half England.
The trade declined with the popularity of
clay roofing tiles; abandoned quarries now
litter the region, some once prosperous
enough to employ hundreds of men.*

   *FFESTINIOG RAILWAY, with its narrow
gauge trains, follows the route that
once took slate to Porthmadog harbour, to
be shipped all over the world.*

   *PENRHYN CASTLE (above), further north
in Gwynedd, is also connected with the
slate industry through Richard Pennant,*

*its owner during the second half of the 18th
century. Pennant put enormous energy
into exploiting the slate quarries in the Nant
Ffrancon valley, developing roads,
building a port and establishing a huge
and wealthy business.*

   *The original castle dates back to the
13th century, but it was transformed into
its present appearance in the 1820s,
when it was redesigned in the neo-Norman
style by Thomas Hopper. Everything
from the battlements to the smallest tables
was built by local workmen as nearly as
possible in the 'Norman' manner. Slate was
used in fireplaces, floors, the Grand
Staircase and, most remarkably, in a bed
weighing a tonne.*

The deep valleys of SNOWDONIA NATIONAL PARK (right), with their still lakes and tumbling waterfalls, add considerably to the charms of the wild region called by the Welsh 'the land of eagles'.

This magnificent park takes in 220,000 ha (845 square miles) of countryside, stretching from Llanberis in the north to the Dovey estuary on Cardigan Bay in the south.

SNOWDON, the 'king of the mountains', rises to 1,085 m (3,560 ft), the highest peak south of the Scottish border. There are many routes to the summit for climbers. One of the most beautiful is the Watkin Path, starting from Nant Gwynant; others include the Miners' Track which begins beside Llyn Llydaw at the top of Llanberis Pass and the challenging Beddgelert Track on the west side. For those who cannot face the climb, there is the steam-operated Snowdon Mountain Railway, with rack and pinion drive, opened in 1896, running from Llanberis to the summit.

CADER IDRIS, the great mass of volcanic rock in the south of the park, has always been a favourite with hill walkers because of its dramatic cliffs, wild rocky slopes and panoramic views from the summit. The name means 'chair of Idris' and though the identity of Idris is unclear, some say that it was another name for King Arthur.

BEDDGELERT, a village locked in by mountains, is one of the most popular centres for exploring Snowdonia. Its name, the 'grave of Gelert', is probably linked to a holy man of the Middle Ages — the legend that it was the grave of Prince Llywelyn's faithful dog was invented by the landlord of a local hotel.

The little medieval church of **LLANDANWG** (right) stands near the water's edge, with sand piled high around it. Over the years, strenuous efforts have been made to reclaim it from the engulfing sand dunes, but the wind always blows the sand back again. It once served as the parish church of Harlech, in Gwynedd, but was replaced by a new building in 1841. The ancient medieval font has been removed to the newer church but Llandanwg still has an inscribed stone that may date from Roman times. The beach nearby is popular with holidaymakers but the water has dangerous currents, created by the River Artro.

WALES

*The l9th-century fort of **St Catherine's Island** (left) was built by Lord Palmerston as part of the defences against a possible French attack. The island can be reached by walking across the sands at low tide from the old walled town of **Tenby,** in Dyfed, which stands on a rocky peninsula with a wide beach on either side and a picturesque harbour.*

*Boats take visitors to **Caldey,** the 'island of saints', a religious centre since the 6th century. The Cistercian community that inhabits the island, raising barley and making the famous Caldey perfume, was founded early this century.*

*The heavily carved door of **Plas Newydd,** Llangollen (below) makes a fitting entrance for the handsome black and white building, once the home of the eccentric 'Ladies of Llangollen', who entertained many celebrated men, including Wordsworth, Sir Walter Scott and the Duke of Wellington.*

ENGLAND'S HEARTLAND

The Midland counties were the cradle of the industrial revolution and England's heart has continued to beat to the throb of heavy machinery, but its pastoral charm is still strong: its fertile lands watered by great rivers, quiet villages showing a wealth of stone, timber and thatch, and the remnants of ancient forests standing firm.

Naunton, in Gloucestershire, is a straggling village set along the deep Windrush valley, its Cotswold stone buildings standing against the rich backcloth of the wold. Its church has a handsome perpendicular tower and many of the houses date from the 17th century, with lovely old gables.

The wide diversity of counties that make up England's heartland often have little but their situation in common, but this is a region as rich in history as in delightful scenery. There is, of course, Stratford-upon-Avon with all its Shakespearean associations, an artistic and literary mecca which draws visitors from every corner of the world. Its prominence as a tourist centre has tended to overshadow even such nearby gems as the vast fortress at Warwick, the romantic medieval ruins of Kenilworth Castle, where Robert Dudley entertained Queen Elizabeth I so lavishly that he was almost bankrupted in the process, and the elegant town of Royal Leamington Spa, its Regency and early Victorian houses dating from its heyday as a fashionable watering place. The Midlands were once the 'cockpit of England', where momentous battles were fought. At Edgehill in Warwickshire, the Royalist forces of the Civil War were victorious in 1642 but three years later they were decisively defeated by Cromwell's troops at Naseby in Northamptonshire. Earlier, at Bosworth Field near Leicester, the Yorkists were finally routed by the Lancastrians, leaving the way open for the establishment of the Tudor dynasty.

Industries past and present have left their scars across the land: the busy steel, iron and brassworks of the Black Country, the coalfields of Derbyshire and Nottinghamshire which formed the background to the novels of D. H. Lawrence, the railway works of Derby, the car factories of Coventry and Birmingham, and the brewing industry of Burton-upon-Trent. The 'five towns' of the Staffordshire Potteries were famous long before Arnold Bennett wrote about them in his novels. Some of the famous names in china — among them Wedgwood, Spode, Copeland, Minton and Royal Doulton — come from this area and have become sought after throughout the world as examples of superb craftsmanship.

However, it would be a mistake to think that England's heart consists of industry. None of the factory sites is far from pleasant countryside: for instance, Birmingham has more canals than Venice, flowing through a wide variety of interesting scenery, both urban and rural, and cheek by jowl with the dismal Black Country sprawl is Cannock Chase, once the hunting ground of royalty, now open to all, a lovely tract of forest, heath and hillside, complete with a large herd of fallow deer. Besides these peaceful oases in the midst of the industrial scene, some counties have large areas of unspoilt countryside, rivalling any of Britain's beauty spots. The rolling limestone hills of the Cotswolds shelter villages of honey-coloured stone which seem to grow naturally out of the landscape. ▷ 92

SNOWSHILL (left) stands on a hill looking out over the Avon valley, near the Cotswold town of Broadway, a huddle of old cottages, a little church and a village green. The 17th- and 18th-century manor house has beautiful terraced gardens and an amazing collection of toys, clocks, musical instruments and other artefacts.

Another of Gloucestershire's fascinating buildings is BERKELEY CASTLE, in the Severn Vale, owned by the same family for 800 years. Built in the 12th century, it contains the cell in which Edward II was murdered in 1327 (right), as well as an impressive 18 m (60 ft) long Great Hall.

DUDDINGTON, where the river Welland flows through a four-arched bridge, is one of Northamptonshire's most picturesque spots. The bridge, the church and the old watermill, built in 1664, are all made from local limestone.

This much neg1ected county has many delightful villages, fine churches and stately houses. Within a few kilometres of Duddington are KING'S CLIFFE, with a Norman church tower and 17th-century almhouses, COTTERSTOCK, with the 17th-century Hall beside the River Nene, where the poet Dryden wrote his Fables in an attic, and FOTHERINGHAY, where the church of St Mary and All Saints has a magnificent octagonal lantern tower. Only a mound remains to mark the site of the old castle. Here, in the banqueting hall, Richard III was born and Mary, Queen of Scots, was executed. She is said to have planted Scotch thistles while she was imprisoned in the castle and they still grow here.

Further south, towards Northampton, are two outstanding houses. KIRBY HALL is a romantic ruin, begun in 1570 and bought shortly afterwards by Christopher Hatton, a favourite of Queen Elizabeth I. It was largely remodelled in the 17th cen-tury by Inigo Jones, who added the palatial north front.

Near Geddington is BOUGHTON HOUSE, originally a Tudor monastic building, enlarged into a palace in the 16th and 17th centuries. The house contains an excellent collection of furniture and china, brought from France in the 17th century by the 1st Duke of Montagu.

In the main square of GEDDINGTON itself is one of the three remaining Eleanor Crosses, marking the stages of the funeral procession of Edward I's queen.

In the Malvern Hills, which rise sharply from level countryside in Hereford and Worcester, Sir Edward Elgar found the inspiration for much of his music and he claimed that his spirit would forever haunt the hillsides. In Gloucestershire the little-known Forest of Dean is one of the largest ancient forests in the country with mighty oaks, ash, birch and conifer. Above all there is the Peak District National Park (named after an ancient British tribe called the Peacs), which offers rugged, rocky walking country with a fascinating underground world of caves and tunnels.

Three very different rivers — the Avon, the Severn and the Wye — flow past many of the most attractive and interesting places in the region. The Avon is ▷ 97

The River Windrush flows through the main street of **Bourton-on-the-Water** *(above), bordered by lawns, shaded by trees and crossed by low bridges. This scene has made the village one of the most popular in the Cotswolds, attracting crowds of summer tourists.*

Nearby are the famous villages of **Upper** *and* **Lower Slaughter**. *Lower Slaughter, where the river runs past mellow stone cottages and under little bridges, is a mecca for artists and photographers. Upper Slaughter has a lovely Elizabethan manor house and the old rectory, now a hotel, where the Reverend F. E. Witts wrote* **The Diary of a Cotswold Parson**.

THE MIDLANDS

At **ROSS-ON WYE** the 17th-century Market Hall (below) dominates the Market Place. The ground floor is open, lined with rows of stately red sandstone pillars and a white stone medallion of Charles II is set between the gables.

Opposite is the Man of Ross House, where lived John Kyrle, a wealthy 17th-century philanthropist who did much for the town, including financing the restoration of the 14th-century spire of St Mary's Church, which rises 63 m (208 ft) into the air. Alexander Pope gave him the name the 'Man of Ross' when he sang his praises in his **Moral Essays**.

One of John Kyrle's legacies to the town was the Prospect, a public walled garden near the church, with excellent views of the river and surrounding hills.

THE MIDLANDS

SYMONDS YAT, meaning 'gate' or 'pass', is the best-known beauty spot of the Wye Valley (right). Here the Wye flows through a narrow, deeply wooded gorge, making an 8 km (5 mile) loop around Huntsham Hill, doubling back on itself to leave a near-island. The best view is from the 144 m (473 ft) Yat Rock, on the Gloucestershire side of the river.

The ruins of **GOODRICH CASTLE** stand nearby, on a hill above the river. Its name was originally Godric's Castle, for its three-storey Norman keep was built in 1160 for Godric Mappestone. It was later enlarged and could be approached only across a deep moat cut in solid rock. It was destroyed by Cromwell's troops in the Civil War, with the help of a cannon called Roaring Meg, which fired 91 kg (200 lb) cannonballs. Roaring Meg can be seen near the cathedral in Hereford.

KILPECK's church of St Mary and St David is a superb example of Norman architecture, with a richly carved south doorway, remarkable in its detail (left). A Tree of Life bears thick bunches of grapes while above it fan out a wide variety of creatures — dragons, birds, snakes and a flying angel. A frieze runs round the outside of the building. with several dozen strange figures. The church was built in the 12th century, on the site of an Anglo-Saxon building.

CHESTERFIELD's crooked church spire has made the town famous. The 69 m (228 ft) octagonal spire has developed a strange twist, probably caused by the reaction of heat and cold on the lead covering the timber frame. The church of St Mary and All Saints, which dates from the 14th century, has graceful proportions. There is a medieval font, medieval screens and some interesting monuments to the Foljambe family dating from the second half of the 16th century. Various chapels within the church were once dedicated to guilds.

a peaceful, civilized river that takes a placid course through highly cultivated countryside. It flows below the walls of Warwick Castle, through the 14 arches of the 15th-century Clopton Bridge at Stratford and the even older eight-arched bridge at Bidford, through the Vale of Evesham, where in spring cherry and apple orchards blanket the fields with fleecy pink and white blossom. At the dignified town of Tewkesbury, with its half-timbered houses and fine Norman abbey, the Avon joins the Severn, robust and powerful. The Severn, called Sabrina by the Romans, flows south into the estuary near Bristol, passing handsome towns such as Bridgnorth, dramatically divided into the High and the Low Town, which are connected by a funicular railway, Bewdley with its many elegant Georgian buildings, and Upton-on-Severn, a delightful spot in itself, and an excellent centre for river cruising. The Wye is a clean, dancing river which rises in the Cambrian Mountains, flows in an enormous wooded loop round Symonds Yat, then runs along the England-Wales border before merging with the Severn below Chepstow. The poet Thomas Gray described the rocky gorges, high woodlands and luxuriant pastures along its banks as 'a succession of nameless beauties'. ▷ **102**

WORCESTER CATHEDRAL (left) stands on the bank of the River Severn, its buildings reflected in the quiet water. The first cathedral was founded by St Oswald in AD 983 but the earliest part of the present cathedral. the crypt, was built by the Saxon bishop Wulfstan, who kept his office by submitting to William the Conqueror. The chapter house was built in the early 12th century anà the choir was designed in the 15th century, but the major part of the building dates from the 14th century.

The cathedral contains King John's effigy and tomb, dating from 1216, and the delicately-carved chapel built to house the tomb of Prince Arthur, son of Henry VII, who died in 1502.

Stokesay Castle (right) in Shropshire, one of England's oldest fortified manor houses, has scarcely changed since the 13th century, when Lawrence of Ludlow, a rich wool merchant, turned an earlier Norman building into a comfortable but well-protected home, building a gabled great hall between two stone towers.

The two buildings above may look like fortified towers but they are not what they seem. *Broadway Tower* (above left) is a folly built by the Earl of Coventry in 1799, so that his family could see it from their Worcestershire estate. It stands on Broadway Hill, which at over 305 m (1,000 ft), is the second highest point in the Cotswolds. The *Triangular Lodge* (above right) in the grounds of Rushton Hall, Northamptonshire, had a more serious purpose. Sir Thomas Tresham designed it in honour of the Holy Trinity: it has three sides with three gables on each and three floors.

IRONBRIDGE GORGE MUSEUM in Shropshire preserves the historic sites of the birth of the Industrial Revolution. The gorge itself, once full of smoke and sulphur fumes, is now green and leafy, though modern cooling towers nearby (left) give some idea of the scene in past centuries.

At **COALBROOKDALE** in 1709 Abraham Darby first used coke instead of charcoal to smelt iron. This was a discovery vital to the iron industry, leading to vast improvements in the production of good quality iron. The rapid expansion of the industry brought riches to the area and forward-looking engineers were drawn here from all over the world.

The world's first iron bridge (above) was built across the Severn in 1777, giving a name to the gorge. It is 61 m (200 ft) long, with a single arch spanning 30 m (100 ft), a magnificent feat of civil engineering for its time and a brave venture for Darby and his workmen, who had to work out methods of casting and transporting the component parts of the enormous structure. The bridge was used for traffic right up to 1931.

The six square miles (15 square kilometres) of the museum take in several major historic sites. At the west end of the gorge, in Coalbrookdale itself, is Darby's original blast furnace and nearby is the Great Warehouse, housing a museum illustrating the development of ironmaking. In the main valley of the Severn is a warehouse, turned into an interpretative centre to tell the story of the area, and the Bedlam blast furnaces.

At **BLISTS HILL**, above Coalport, a fascinating collection of buildings and industrial exhibits has been assembled, and peopled by staff in period costume, to give a vivid glimpse of past history: it includes a tollhouse designed by Thomas Telford, a 19th-century print shop, a blacksmith's forge and a chemist's shop.

Several of the most impressive cathedrals in the country grace the Midlands counties. Hereford has been the seat of a bishop since AD 672, though the cathedral is mainly Norman, with later additions. It has a rare medieval library, with books chained to the wall and the ancient Mappa Mundi, drawn in the 14th century when the earth was thought to be flat, with Jerusalem at its centre. Worcester Cathedral preserves the crypt built by Bishop Wulfstan in 1084, and almost untouched since his day. Coventry has a cathedral of a very different style. In 1940 one of the most disastrous bombing raids of World War II devastated the major part of the city, leaving the Cathedral Church of St Michael in ruins. The 91 m (300 ft) spire and part of the walls remain, adjoining the new Cathedral designed by Sir Basil Spence and completed in 1962. The rosy sandstone of the exterior is cut on Gothic lines: inside, the long windows in vivid reds, greens, yellows and

HADDON HALL (below) is a romantic, rambling old house standing on the banks of the Derbyshire Wye. The original building dates from the 11th century and though much of the present hall is 16th century, it has kept many of its medieval walls and rooms.

The famous story of the 16th-century elopement of Dorothy Vernon, daughter of the hall's owner Sir George Vernon, with John Manners, has all the trappings of romantic fiction. She is said to have fled down the steps just off the long gallery, during her sister's wedding party, to meet her lover at the packhorse bridge (right). The story has been embellished over the years, as the long gallery and the adjoining section of the garden were built many years later.

blues throw panels of coloured light the length of the building. Above the altar is the 23 m (75 ft) tapestry by Graham Sutherland, *Christ in Glory*.

The villages of the heartland of England have fascinating names like Upton Snodsbury, Much Marcle, Potters Crouch, Shipton-under-Wychwood and even the imposing Ruyton-of-the-Eleven-Towns, which gained its name in the 14th century with the amalgamation of 11 townships. Some, like Bibury in Gloucestershire, with its river bridges and 17th-century cottages, are among the most beautiful in England; others, like Welford-on-Avon in Warwickshire, with timber-framed houses and a maypole on the green, would merit any 'best kept village' award. Many age-old customs have survived in this region, like the Easter Bottle-Kicking in Leicestershire, where young men from two rival villages, Hallaton and Medbourne, scramble for the bottles, or small casks of beer, each team trying to carry them over a brook into their own parish. At Atherstone in Warwickshire, a football game that originated in the 13th century is played in the streets on Shrove Tuesday. Villages throughout Derbyshire including Tissington, Wormhill and Eyam 'dress' their wells with tapestry-like flower pictures once a year, in a ceremony that may go back to the pagan custom of propitiating the water gods, though some say it originated at the time of the Black Death. At Abbot's Bromley in Staffordshire the 'deer men' taking part in the September Horn Dance process round the town bearing antlers thought to be 1,000 years old, performing a dance dating back to prehistoric times. □

Derbyshire has a wide variety of attractions for the visitor: the wild countryside of the Peak District, with its crags and caverns, the beauties of the Dales and magnificent stately homes.

WINNATS PASS, near Castleton, is an awesome ravine leading out of the Hope Valley (left). Since landslides from Mam Tor, the 'Shivering Mountain', closed the main road, traffic has been diverted along the steep and narrow pass. Below the pass lies Speedwell Cavern, one of many vast underground caves in the region, which can only be approached by boat, along a channel made by lead miners 200 years ago.

CHATSWORTH (below) is one of England's great country houses, built in the late 17th century for the 1st Duke of Devonshire. Its elegant interior has fine paintings, sculpture and furniture, while the gardens, the work of Joseph Paxton, who designed the Crystal Palace, have spectacular fountains.

THE BIG SKY COUNTRY

*The very pace of life seems
slower in East Anglia, where
the watery expanses of
broads and marshes alternate
with great tracts of rich,
dark farmland. There is a
special quality of light here,
a clarity and brilliance
that has moved great artists
to capture the country
scenes on canvas.*

*At Horsey Mere reeds are regularly cut back to
prevent the open water of the broad reverting to fen.
Only sand dunes separate it from the North Sea
and salt water seeps in, making the water brackish, so
that the plant and animal life is unusual.*

There is an impression of endless space about East Anglia, with its uncluttered horizons, great patchwork panoramas of pastureland and huge stretches of shallow mere and marsh, the ground seldom rising more than 91 m (300 ft) above sea level. The sky is an integral part of the landscape here: sometimes a clear, luminous blue, sometimes a windswept vista of scudding clouds, often spectacular at sunrise and sunset.

The countryside has proved to be the inspiration of several great artists, chief among them John Constable, born in the Suffolk village of East Bergholt. The busy market town of Sudbury was the birthplace of Thomas Gainsborough, better known for his portraits but also skilled as a landscape painter. His family's Tudor house is now a museum and art centre. John Crome (known as 'Old' Crome to distinguish him from his artist son) was the founder of the Norwich School, concentrating on the scenery of his native Norfolk and using techniques derived from Dutch painters. While artists have left pictorial records of the rural East Anglia of the 18th century, others have captured its various moods in equally lasting forms. The poet George Crabbe was

AUDLEY END (below), in Essex, was a family home for 400 years. Various owners altered, demolished and rebuilt the house, so that only part of the 17th-century structure built by the Earl of Suffolk, Lord High Treasurer of England, still remains.

Though it is still one of the largest stately homes in Britain, the house was originally twice the present size. Much of it was demolished in the 18th century on the advice of Sir John Vanburgh, who added the stone screen in the Great Hall and the double staircase with its handsome plaster ceiling. Robert Adam remodelled several rooms on the ground floor, though alterations were made in the 19th century.

Lancelot 'Capability' Brown landscaped the grounds in the 1760s, adding ornamental buildings, including a Palladian bridge and the Temple of Concord, built to commemorate George III's recovery from his first attack of insanity.

born in Aldeburgh, Suffolk, in 1754, and his word pictures of country life are full of realistic detail. From one of his works came the idea for Benjamin Britten's opera **Peter Grimes,** which captures the angry mood of the storm-battered Suffolk coast. Since 1948 Aldeburgh's annual music festival has brought the town an international reputation as a centre for the arts. To this day, the region has more than its share of artists, musicians and craftsmen, many of them refugees from a hostile urban environment, seeking the tranquillity of villages that still seem untouched by the modern world.

For centuries the sea-bordered counties of Norfolk and Suffolk (the North Folk and the South Folk), East Anglia proper, were separated from the rest of Britain by thick forests in the south and the watery wastelands of the fens in the west. Those who travelled the length

EPPING FOREST stretches from the town of Epping in the north to Wanstead in the south, its 2,428 ha (6,000 acres) the last remnant of the favourite hunting ground of English kings for 600 years. Though it is now tiny compared to its past size, it still seems suprisingly extensive.

It was purchased for the public by the Corporation of London in 1882 and formally opened by Queen Victoria. Later she wrote in her diary that the 'Park has been given to the poor of the East End as a sort of recreation ground'. She appointed her son Arthur, Duke of Connaught, as Ranger and Connaught Water (above) was named after him.

of the country had no cause to branch off into England's eastern 'bulge'. Successive influxes of immigrants and invaders swept in from the sea – the Angles from Holstein, their numbers so great that the region became known as 'Angle-land', the Vikings, and then in the 14th century the Flemish weavers, who established the prosperous wool trade. In the Middle Ages, this was one of the most populous parts of the country and the legacy of these wealthy days remains in the handsome timber-framed houses of towns such as Lavenham and Bildeston, the unspoilt Guildhall at Hadleigh and the Old Moot Hall at Sudbury. Above all, there are the hundreds of medieval churches. something like 450 in Suffolk and over 600 in Norfolk. Many, like the 15th century St Peter and St Paul at Salle and St Mary's at Kersey, mentioned in the Domesday Book, are magnificent buildings, now well out of proportion to the size of the communities they serve.

As the forests disappeared and the fens were drained at last in the 17th century, the boundaries of East Anglia became more elastic, so that it now takes in Essex, Cambridgeshire and Lincolnshire. The Romans, who made a first unsuccessful attempt at draining the fens, had established a settlement at Colchester long before London was developed, building on a site occupied as early as the Bronze Age, while Lincoln grew up as a fortified camp at the junction of two Roman roads. Cambridge, at the crossing of the River Cam, was an important strategic site in Roman times, but the beginnings of today's prestigious seat of learning came in the 13th century, with the founding of the first college, Peterhouse, in 1284 by the Bishop of Ely, Hugh de Balsham. Most of the colleges were founded between the 14th and the 16th centuries, among them King's College, founded by Henry VI in 1441, and Queens' College, founded in 1448 by Henry VI's wife Margaret and refounded in 1465 by Edward IV's wife Elizabeth.

For many visitors, the famous broads are the chief magnet of East Anglia. The broads were once thought to be a natural phenomenon, lakes left behind by a receding sea in the long-distant past, but modern research has established that they are man-made. Medieval peat-diggers excavated dozens of pits, as they

*The amazing **LAYER MARNEY TOWER** (left), in Essex, stands 24 m (80 ft) high, dominating the flat surrounding countryside. Built by Henry, 1st Lord Marney, in 1520, it was planned as the gatehouse to a much grander house, but within five years both Lord Marney and his son were dead and the building was never completed.*

The design of the double set of towers, the exterior with eight storeys and the interior with seven, was much influenced by the current Italian style of architecture, with the lavish use of terracotta. The towers are crowned by decorative scallop shells and dolphins.

***SALING HALL** is almost as old as Layer Marney but its pleasing walled garden (above) was laid out in the late 17th century. The current owner has restored and improved the grounds, adding new touches such as the Japanese garden.*

111

gathered fuel for the growing city of Norwich. With the general rise in sea level the pits were then flooded. Over the centuries, fishermen and reed-cutters opened up channels between them and into nearby rivers so that the Broads as we know them were born. Their history explains why they are often below the level of even the flattest surrounding countryside, so that, from a distance, the sails of passing boats appear to be gliding through the fields. The best way to see the Broads is by boat, and Wroxham and Horning are the most popular places for sailing. Woodland and water gardens border South Walsham Broad. Ranworth Broad has a nature trail through the reeds and fen and Hickling is known for its diving ducks. Though the Broads can become overcrowded and noisy in summer, at the end of the season they revert to peace and stillness, the only sound the ducks quacking contentedly in the reeds.

The wild stretches of East Anglia's country and coast are dotted with nature reserves and bird sanctuaries.

WILLY LOTT'S COTTAGE (below) on the tree-shaded banks of the River Stour has changed little since John Constable painted it in the early 19th century. Constable's father owned nearby Flatford Mill and here he spent much of his boyhood. Though neither mill nor cottage are open to the public, the scenes that provided the artist with inspiration attract crowds of tourists, trying to guess exactly where he sat while painting.

Constable's birthplace was the village of EAST BERGHOLT and he wrote: 'I love every stile and stump and lane in the village; as long as I am able to hold a brush I shall never cease to paint them.' His parents are buried in St Mary's churchyard, which has a belltower where bells hang upside down and are rung by hand, without the aid of ropes.

Holme-next-the-Sea, on the Norfolk coast, is a place of dunes, salt marshes and mud flats, where a wide variety of migrating birds can be seen in autumn, as they pass through on their way south from the Arctic. In the reedy marshes and heathlands of Minsmere in Suffolk more than 100 species breed every year: from the hides visitors can see herons and terns, spoonbills and even the rare avocet. The marshy flats of Norfolk's Blakeney Point make popular nesting grounds and in winter, when the area between the Old and New Bedford Rivers in Cambridgeshire is flooded, it provides a home for pintails, gadwalls, Bewick's and Whooper swans and a large variety of wintering wildfowl. The pattern of bird migration is studied at the field station at Gibraltar Point in Lincolnshire, where tracks ▷ 123

Below **FRAMLINGHAM CASTLE** *in Suffolk is an old mere, its marshy vegetation bright with yellow flag iris (above) preserved as a nature reserve. The castle, seen here in misty outline, was begun in the 12th century by Hugh Bigod, the 1st Earl of Norfolk, but rebuilt in the early 13th century, with 13 towers around its mighty walls.*

St MICHAEL'S CHURCH, in the village, contains tombs of the Howard family, formerly in Thetford Priory. The tomb of the Duke of Richmond, bastard son of Henry VIII, has carvings of scenes from Genesis and Exodus, while that of Thomas, 3rd Duke of Norfolk, has figures of the Apostles.

The colleges and chapels of **CAMBRIDGE UNIVERSITY** are some of the most exquisite buildings in East Anglia.

The Grand Court of **TRINITY COLLEGE** (far left) lays claim to being the largest university court in the world. The Renaissance fountain dates from 1602 and much of the court was designed by a 17th-century Master of the College.

KING'S COLLEGE CHAPEL (above with Clare College) is recognized as one of the most magnificent Gothic buildings in Europe. Begun in 1446 by Henry VI, it was not completed until the early 16th century.

THE BRIDGE OF SIGHS (left) was built in 1831 to connect New Court with the older buildings of St John's College. Though its real name is New Bridge, it has always been called after the famous 16th-century bridge in Venice.

At *SHINGLE STREET*, *near Hollesley in Suffolk, a row of coastguard cottages stands above a bank of shingle thrown up by heavy seas (right). Among the interesting seashore flowers is the sea kale. In the past, young shoots of sea kale were eaten as a vegetable and it was well known that these could be made more tender if shingle was mounded round each plant to blanch it.*

LAVENHAM (left), in Suffolk, owes its unique collection of medieval buildings to its heyday as a prosperous wool town, famous for its blue cloth. The inhabitants were wealthy enough to build substantial timbered houses at a time when timber was both scarce and expensive.

The GUILDHALL, in Market Place, dates from the 1530s, soon after the founding of the Guild of Corpus Christi, one of three guilds prominent in the wool industry. Since then it has been used as a prison, a workhouse, a court and a school. Now owned by the National Trust, it houses a museum. The town has a wealth of handsome exteriors, among them the 15th-century Little Hall in Market Place and Schilling Hall, several houses in Church Street and notable old inns like the Angel and the Swan, which incorporates the Old Wool Hall.

Rivalries between wool towns were fierce, and the people of Lavenham were determined that their church should have the grandest of all towers. It rises 43 m (141 ft), dwarfing the rest of the church of ST PETER AND ST PAUL, and was mainly financed by a rich clothier, Thomas Spring, whose son was so proud of his brand-new coat of arms that he had it depicted over 30 times on the top of the tower. Inside the church is the tomb of Spring and his wife Alice, with a beautifully carved 16th-century parclose screen, probably executed by Flemish craftsmen.

PARGETING, the art of carving plasterwork into patterns and raised ornamental pictures, is a decorative technique in Essex and Suffolk, dating from Elizabethan times. As the cost of timber rose steeply, plaster was used to cover wood framing, which was less expensive. Good examples can be seen on several houses at Coggeshall, on the river Blackwater in Essex. The Ancient House in Ipswich, a fine Jacobean example, has coloured pargeting. Near the church in Clare, Suffolk, is a 15th-century house that once belonged to the priest, with intricate floral designs an its walls and gable-ends.

EAST ANGLIA

OVERY STAITHE, once a bustling port, is now a quiet little boating harbour, just downstream from the village of Burnham Overy in Norfolk. The village, on the river Burn, has a three storey water mill, dating from the late 18th century and a group of well-preserved mill buildings, including the barn, maltings and miller's house, all under the care of the National Trust. Nearby is a wooden windmill of the early 19th century. St Clement's Church has a Norman tower capped by a 17th-century cupola.

The elegant Custom House at **KING'S LYNN**, Norfolk, built in 1683, stands overlooking the Purfleet, a reminder of the town's important trading past (above). It was designed by Henry Bell, a successful local architect who was twice mayor of the town. A niche on the north side has a statue of Charles II.

Another of King's Lynn's frequently photographed buildings is the Guildhall, with a striking flint chessboard design. It was built in 1421 and an Elizabethan extension was added in the same style.

One of the outstanding sights of **ELY CATHEDRAL**, in Cambridgeshire, is the Octagon, a giant eight-sided lantern tower built by Alan de Walsingham in 1322 after the Tower of the original Norman

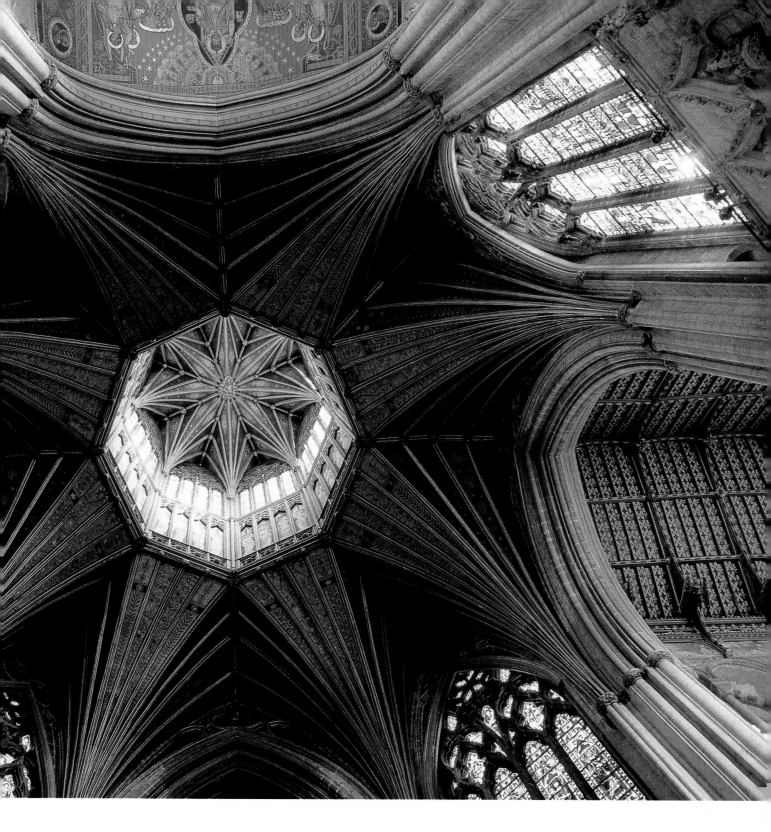

building collapsed. With its fan vaulting and delicate tracery (above) it is not only a glorious piece of architecture but also one of the wonders of medieval engineering, as the structure supports more than 400 tonnes of masonry.

The cathedral, which dominates the flat fen landscape for great distances, was built in 1083 on the site of a 7th-century Benedictine monastery. The nave, with its Norman columns and painted wooden ceilings, is 164 m (537 ft) long. The 14th-century choir stalls have excellent carvings and the elaborately decorated roofs of the chapels are very memorable, particularly that of the Lady Chapel completed in 1349 under the supervision of John of Wisbech.

East Anglia is one of Britain's most productive agricultural regions. Bales of corn neatly stacked across huge fields (above) show the efficiency of modern methods but there has been a price to pay: small farms have been swallowed up by larger holdings, and many woods and hedges have disappeared.

Once wind pumps were an essential part of the drainage system of the fens and hundreds could be seen working busily. Now there are few survivors, like the mill which has been restored to working order at **WICKEN FEN**, in Cambridgeshire (left), a

lead through an expanse of salt marsh and dunes.

The people of East Anglia have always prided themselves on being rugged, hardy folk with a tough independence of spirit. This was the homeland of the formidable tribe of Iceni, who, led by Boadicea, sacked the Roman settlement at Colchester in an uprising in AD 60 and came near to driving the Roman legions from the region. Bury St Edmunds is known as the 'Cradle of the Law', for it was here that a group of barons swore on the altar of St Edmund in 1215 that they would force King John to sign the Magna Carta, and so changed the course of history. Improving communications, a rising population and the increased prosperity of east coast ports, which have benefited from the decline of London's docks, means that East Anglia is being inexorably drawn towards the rest of Britain, so that few of the North and South Folk still refer to incomers as 'foreigners'. In future, the region may lose some of its attractive remoteness but it is unlikely to lose its sturdy character. □

nature reserve covering an undrained remnant of the once extensive marshes.

***HEACHAM** in Norfolk is famed for its fields of sweet-smelling lavender, which has been dried and distilled into scents and toilet waters here since 1932 (right). Many varieties, in a range of colours, are grown over 40 ha (100 acres). The crop is at its peak in July and early August, when it is harvested ready for processing. Caley Mill, an early 19th century watermill on the site of an older mill dating back 900 years, is the home of Norfolk lavender. Visitors can take a guided tour and buy products from the mill shop.*

EAST ANGLIA

From the rolling chalk uplands of the
LINCOLNSHIRE WOLDS *there are extensive*
views over the Bain valley (right) and,
from the highest points, glimpses of Lincoln
Cathedral and the 14th-century Boston
Stump, the tower of St Botolph's Church
on the River Witham. The smooth curves
of the chalk hills shelter secret wooded
valleys and dreaming villages, seemingly
undisturbed by modern noise and rush.

SOMERSBY, at the southern end of the
wolds, was the birthplace of Alfred, Lord
Tennyson, who wrote lovingly of the calm
and peace of the countryside.

MISSIONARIES, MARAUDERS, MOORS AND MILLS

The mighty backbone of the Pennines and the high, grassy domes of the Cheviots are the crowning glory of the north-east countryside which flattens out into a patchwork of farmland on the Humberside coast. The streams from the broad moors once provided energy for the 'dark satanic mills' of the industrial revolution.

The flat golden farmland of Humberside, the new county which replaced the old East Riding of Yorkshire, is in great contrast to the wild, rugged moors of North Yorkshire and the infinitely varied character of the Yorkshire Dales.

Though in modern times Yorkshire and Northumbria, taking in Durham, Cleveland and Northumberland, seem so separate and so distinct from each other, in ancient times the Saxon kingdom of Northumbria extended over the whole region, ruled by Anglo-Saxon monarchs who took over after the departure of the Romans. It was a time of turmoil and bloodshed, of warring with rival kings of Mercia and Wessex and fierce fighting with the Picts from north of the border. It was also the time of the blossoming of Christianity, beginning with the arrival of an Irish monk called Aidan, sent by St Columba from Iona. He set up a monastery on the island of Lindisfarne, now known as Holy Island, and from here the Christian mission spread until it reached far enough south to link with the conversion work begun by St Augustine in Canterbury, fanning out to embrace the whole country.

The region is full of reminders that for centuries Christianity and violence existed side by side. The monks of Holy Island were forced to flee from Viking invaders in the 9th century, taking with them the body of the 7th-century bishop St Cuthbert. After 200 years the saint was eventually laid to rest at Durham, which became a centre of pilgrimage, and his community of monks were re-established as Benedictines. Nothing remains of the earliest church built here: the present cathedral was begun in 1093 by Bishop William of Calais, high on the pinnacle of rock above the river Wear which it shares with the Norman castle, an important stronghold of the conquerors. The prince bishops of Durham wielded enormous temporal and ecclesiastical power and were as ready to fight in hand-to-hand battle as to attend to their religious affairs.

One of the most revered religious shrines is St Paul's Church, Jarrow, part of the monastery where the Venerable Bede lived and worked on the earliest written history of England. It was Bede who first described Hadrian's Wall, then already 600 years old, built to repulse northern raiders. In Norman times, the need to maintain order led to the building of other castles besides Durham: Bamburgh replaced an

COUNTY ARCADE (left) in Leeds, designed by Frank Matcham, has been restored to its Victorian splendour, using expertise gained from the Great Western Arcade, Birmingham and the Burlington Arcade, London. Six of the original mahogany shopfronts remained, and the rest have been restored in the same style. Together with Victoria Street, which has been roofed over with stained glass, it is known as the Victorian Quarter of the city.

NEEDLE'S EYE (above), a pyramid pierced by an arch, is a folly built in the grounds of Wentworth Woodhouse, near Rotherham, in the 1780s. The owner of the estate boasted that he could drive his horse and carriage through the eye of a needle and then had to build a needle's eye to prove it.

Anglo-Saxon fortress, Alnwick became an impressive stronghold and Norham, built in 1121, was besieged, damaged and restored over the following centuries. In the 14th century, a period of increased border unrest, came another round of castle building. Raby Castle acquired its battlements and reinforcements, Dunstanburgh rose as a mighty fortress on an invincible rock cliff above the sea, and Chillingham grew from an original peel tower. Today, Chillingham's claim to fame is totally peaceful: its main attraction is the herd of wild white cattle, the descendants of wild oxen who roamed the Cheviot foothills. In the 13th century the park was enclosed and a herd was trapped inside. It was only in the 17th and 18th centuries, once the crowns of England and Scotland were joined under the Stuarts and the threat from the north disappeared, that many of the castles were transformed into elegant houses. Alnwick was restored by Robert Adam for the 1st Duke of Northumberland, Chillingham was remodelled and Sir John Vanbrugh designed some fine rooms at Lumley in 1721.   ▷ **134**

WHITBY ABBEY (right), now a gaunt ruin, stands high above the River Esk in north Yorkshire, on the spot where St Hilda founded the first abbey in AD 657, at the request of King Oswy of Northumberland, who had sworn to establish 12 new monasteries in thanks for his victories in battle. The monastery housed both men and women and became a famous seat of learning; five of the early bishops were educated there.

In AD 867, the Danes destroyed St Hilda's abbey. It was refounded in 1087 but the Norman building has also disappeared and the present ruin dates from the 13th century. There is little trace of the monastic buildings.

Ammonites, the coiled fossil stones found below the cliff, are known as 'St Hilda's snakes'. Legend says that she ordered all the snakes in the area over the edge of the cliffs, to curl up and turn to stone below.

SCARBOROUGH *is a bracing North Sea resort with a beautiful natural setting, its two sheltered sandy bays separated by a headland crowned by an ancient castle. Though it was once a well-known spa, no one goes to drink the waters any longer but the town still has much to offer. The harbour (far left) preserves the atmosphere of a busy fishing port and above it narrow stepped passages run up the steep hillside. Visitors who tire of the souvenir shops and amusement arcades can escape for walks along the cliffs or even a peaceful wander in one of the well-kept local churchyards (left).*

The castle has a 13th-century barbican and a keep built in 1168. The curtain walls suffered in many attacks, chief among them the siege by the Parliamentarians from February 1644 to July 1645, when starvation finally forced the Royalists to surrender.

MALHAM COVE (right), seen from the Pennine Way in Airedale, is a great limestone amphitheatre with cliffs 91 m (300 ft) high. At the top is an extraordinary limestone pavement; blocks of rock worn smooth over the centuries, with clefts carved by the action of water, now filled by ferns and other plants. Once the River Aire cascaded over the edge of Malham Cove but now it flows underground.

The 'Great Scar' limestone country of the region, with its line of steep cliffs (below), has been created by the Mid Craven Fault, an ancient fracture in the earth's crust.

MALHAM TARN, further up the valley, is a 61 ha (150 acre) lake, formed by melting glaciers during the Ice Age. The Tarn is part of a nature reserve and field study centre and is an excellent spot for bird watching.

At much the same time, Yorkshire was acquiring some of its splendid great houses. Newby Hall, near Ripon, is a beautiful little Adam house, specially designed to house the collection of classical statuary acquired by the owner in Italy. Robert Adam also added a wing to Nostell Priory, near Wakefield, built 30 years earlier in the grand Palladian style by James Paine, on the site of an Augustinian priory. Capability Brown laid out the park surrounding Sledmere House on Humberside, built in 1751 for the famous Sykes family, whose tireless work did much to beautify the Yorkshire countryside, as well as building and enhancing many of the local churches. The huge and splendid Castle Howard, outside York, was begun by Vanbrugh in 1702 and was still under construction while he was working on Blenheim Palace. By the time the building and decoration were completed 38 years later both Vanbrugh and the 3rd Earl of Carlisle, who commissioned it, were dead. ▷ 139

THE BUTTERTUBS (above) are a series of limestone shafts in the fell-side varying between 15 m and 30 m (50-100 ft) deep, formed by the action of water and frost. They give their name to the Buttertubs Pass between Wensleydale and Swaledale, one of the highest roads in the country, often snowbound in winter.

At the northern end of the dale the River Swale flows beneath the bridge at RICHMOND (right), a market town since the 12th century. Its Norman castle was begun by Alan the Red, but the 30 m (100 ft) keep was built more than a century later,

The medieval alleys, cobbled marketplace and remains of ancient walls make Richmond a historian's delight. The Georgian Theatre Royal was built in 1788 and is preserved in almost its original state.

SWALEDALE (left) is the most northerly of Yorkshire's great dales, its fierce river rushing through thickly wooded ravines, heather-covered slopes and hay meadows. The hardy black-faced Swaledale sheep graze on the hills; the breed may have originated back in Viking times and can withstand the cold of the long, hard winters.

Lead mining flourished here from the 16th century to the late 19th century and mining debris still covers many of the fell-sides. The ruins of the Old Gang mining complex, once one of the busiest and best known, can be seen above Gunnerside village, including the old smelting and crushing mills. The mines themselves are unsafe. **REETH**, an ancient settlement mentioned in the Domesday Book, was something of a boom town in the heyday of lead mining and now houses the Swaledale Folk Museum, which records the rise and decline of the industry.

Less well-known dale country is the **LUNE VALLEY** and its pretty little side dales, where the fells are honeycombed with caves and potholes.

CLAPHAM (below), its whitewashed and grey stone cottages lining a twinkling brook, is a good centre for potholers who aim to explore Gaping Gill, where an underground waterfall links with 15 km (9 miles) of passages and Britain's largest underground cavern.

The Industrial Revolution changed the face of large areas of the north-east. There had been miners searching for lead, silver and zinc in Northumbria since Roman times, but in the 19th century the demand for coal was so enormous that pitheads, slagheaps and miners' cottages proliferated around every likely seam. Coal needed transport, so the railway system grew and expanded. The export prospects of the booming coal industry gave a boost to shipbuilding, shipyards sprawled over the banks of the Tyne and by the late 1880s, eight out of ten ships launched throughout the world came from British yards. In Yorkshire, the advent of steam power meant that the woollen industry moved northwards, nearer to the sources of coal, and in many previously pastoral areas the noise of mill machinery began to fill the valleys. Yorkshire's past is written along the rivers Aire, Colne and Calder, with their grey mill towns and towering chimneys.

DURHAM CATHEDRAL (left), built as a shrine for the body of St Cuthbert, is probably Europe's finest Norman building. It was the first cathedral to use a vaulted roof for the nave. Behind the high altar is the Neville Screen, dating from 1375, magnificently carved from Caen stone. It shields the tomb of St Cuthbert and the saint's relics are displayed in the Treasury Museum.

Over a century after St Cuthbert's body arrived in Durham, the remains of St Oswin were brought to TYNEMOUTH PRIORY, founded by the Benedictines on the site of an Anglo-Saxon monastery. The buildings that remain are mainly 13th century. The little Percy Chapel, with its intricately sculptured roof (below) was added in 1450.

The two castles of **ALNWICK** (right) and **WARKWORTH** (below) were both strongholds of the Percys, the chief family of Northumberland. The Percys have figured prominently in English history since Sir Henry de Percy was created 1st Earl of Northumberland by Henry II in 1377.

ALNWICK CASTLE, the massive grey fortress beside the River Aln, was begun in 1135, and has belonged to the Percy family since 1309. The 1st Earl reconstructed the keep and the Constable's Tower and strengthened the castle to withstand siege by invaders from across the border, though the menacing stone soldiers decorating the battlements were only added in the l9th century .

The first fortification at **WARKWORTH** was built by Robert de Mowbray in the 11th century and a number of additions were made over the next 300 years before it came into the hands of the Percys. They made it their main home, keeping Alnwick chiefly as a defensive fortress, and added the keep and the chapel in the early 15th century.

Once defending the border between England and Scotland was no longer necessary, Alnwick was neglected and began to fall into ruin. After the death of the 11th Earl in 1670, the same fate befell Warkworth, which today remains an imposing ruin.

Alnwick underwent two full-scale restorations, the second in 1854, and its interior is now richly decorated in the classical style of the Italian Renaissance. There are paintings by Canaletto, Van Dyke and Titian, and visitors can tour the dungeons, the armoury and the keep as well as the main apartments.

Yet, in spite of the industries that swallowed up whole belts of towns and cities, an astounding amount of countryside remained unscathed. Yorkshire is famed above all for its dales — a name that came from the Viking word for valleys — where rivers rushing down from the high moorlands have carved their way through the limestone. Each dale has its own particular character. Swaledale is steep and rocky, Wensleydale open and grassy, Nidderdale is unpredictable as the river flows through flat farmlands, under fantastically shaped rocks and through a deep gorge, while Farndale is a famous beauty spot in spring when the banks of the river are covered in daffodils. Above the dales stretches the high plateau of the moors, extending from the Vale of York to the sea and glorious with heather ranging in colour from gentle lavender to deep purple. Something like 1,610 km (1,000 miles) of paths and bridleways explore this world of peace and solitude, with its ancient burial mounds, stone crosses and packhorse trails. For those who want to explore the moors without hiking, vintage steam engines haul the carriages of the North Yorkshire Moors Railway on a 29 km (18 mile) journey from Grosmont in Eskdale, across Goathland Moor and along Newtondale to the market town of Pickering.

Yorkshire's coastline is sometimes called the 'forgotten coast', though it was at Scarborough that

the craze for sea bathing first started in the 19th century. Robin Hood's Bay is said to be the last resting place of the notorious outlaw; falling sick after he had taken refuge at Whitby with two of his followers, he shot three arrows in the air and asked to be buried wherever they landed. The houses of the Bay cling precariously to the cliffside and the streets are often only wide enough to allow a fisherman with a basket on his back to pass through. It was once one of the most active smuggling centres in Britain, with contraband being taken along tunnels under the cottages to be carried off across the moors. This coast is Captain Cook country; the great 18th-century explorer was born at the village of Marton in Cleveland, now a suburb of Middlesborough, and served his apprenticeship in Whitby, where his statue stands on West Cliff, gazing out across the stretch of sea where he first learned the skills of navigation that were to take him round the world. □

LINDISFARNE CASTLE tops a rocky crag on Holy Island (left), overlooking the harbour. Built in 1550 for defensive purposes, it was transformed into a comfortable home by Sir Edwin Lutyens in 1903.

The island was a centre of Christianity from the earliest times, when St Aidan established a monastery in AD 635. The Danes destroyed the original building, but the ruins of the 11th-century Benedictine priory still stand.

BAMBURGH CASTLE (above) already existed when St Aidan arrived on Holy Island: King Ida built his stronghold on a crag of the Great Whin Sill in AD 547 and here the kings of Northumbria were crowned. The Normans rebuilt it in stone, but it owes its present appearance to restoration work in the 18th and 19th centuries.

THE NORTH-EAST

HADRIAN'S WALL was built as a permanent frontier to divide the Romans from the barbarians to the north, marking the limit of the empire. The Emperor Hadrian, visiting Britain after a major uprising of the northern tribes, decided that consolidation would be a wiser course than further expansion. Previously the frontier had been marked by a line of forts, connected by the road later called the Stanegate, but in AD 122, work on the great defensive barrier of the wall was begun.

Construction was carried out by legions under the control of Aulus Platorius Nepos, and began from east of the modern Newcastle upon Tyne. Eventually it stretched for 80 Roman miles (118 m/73½ modern miles) to Bowness, west of Carlisle, its height about 6 m (20 ft) and its width about 3 m (9 ft). To the north was a wide ditch as an extra defence. Seventeen forts were built along the wall, with mile-castles for patrols, and it was manned by 5,500 cavalry and 13,000 infantry.

HOUSESTEADS, or Vercovicium in Roman times, is the best preserved of the forts. It is perched on the steep side of the Whin Sill ridge and stretches over 2 ha (5 acres). It once housed 1,000 Roman troops and contained barracks, a forge, hospital, granary and bakery. A village grew up around the fort with married quarters, shops and temples.

VINDOLANDA was one of the forts of the original line of defences, built some 40 years before the wall, and was the base for 500 soldiers. The headquarters building, with offices, tribunal, shrine and courtyard, and the bathhouse with its central heating system, are well-preserved and fascinating. The museum has an excellent collection of Roman remains and reconstructions explaining the life of the fort.

SUBLIME LAKES AND INDUSTRIAL STRENGTH

The magical scenery of Cumbria is the glorious crown of the north-west, its austere crags and enchanting lakes fashioned during the Ice Age. The majestic mountains of Lakeland contrast with the level Cheshire plain, dotted with historic gems, and the robust cities which grew out of the 19th-century industrial revolution.

Views over Derwentwater in Cumbria emphasize one of the great charms of the Lake District: the juxtaposition of gentle landscape with the wild background of the fells, the peaceful water below a dramatic sky. Ruskin's favourite viewpoint was Friar's Crag, at the edge of the lake.

England's north-west strip takes in a heterogeneous set of counties with widely differing claims for attention. The jewel of the collection is Cumbria, with breathtaking lakes and the highest mountains in England. Then there is Lancashire, with a coastline of famous resorts and much-neglected inland beauties, busy, high-profile Merseyside and prosperous Cheshire, known for its cheese and its black and white houses.

The Lake District acts as a magnet for walkers, climbers, and above all motorists, but when the narrow roads and mountain passes are clogged with traffic, it is still possible to escape into solitude on the rugged fells. The area is small, only some 48 km (30 miles) across, but within its boundaries are 100 peaks over 600 m (2,000 ft), 16 lakes and 10 spectacular waterfalls. The landscape was shaped over many thousands of years: initially, rocks beneath a warm sea were thrown upwards by volcanic eruption during one of the mountain-building phases and rose to a dome that eventually cracked. Glaciers deepened the cracks into valleys and Lakeland began to evolve into its present form. When the ice melted, it deposited large amounts of rock debris; this had the effect of damming water, which collected in deep rock basins or smaller hollows, and the lakes as we know them, came into being.

Its beauties remained little known and unfrequented until the early 19th century, when a young man called William Wordsworth, born and brought up in Lakeland, published his A *Guide through the District of the Lakes*. He wrote that the district was 'capable of satisfying the most intense cravings for the tranquil and the lovely and the perfect to which man, the noblest of her creatures, is subject'. Throughout his long life, Wordsworth was to glorify and romanticize the Lake District, describing its hills, its valleys and its flowers in such loving detail that even now, every scene seems to echo his evocative lines. Many other literary figures succumbed to the lure of the lakes: Southey lived at Greta Hall in Keswick for 40 years and De Quincey at Nab Cottage on Rydal Water. Coleridge, too, was here for several years. Shelley came for a time after his marriage and Charles Lamb was a frequent visitor. The Victorians, whose craving for the

Cheshire is a county whose fascination lies not in spectacular scenery, but in its historical heritage, existing side by side with the rapid changes of modern development.

LITTLE MORETON HALL (above) is one of its most famous sights, a beautiful black and white house scarcely changed since the mid-16th century. Its half-timbered walls lean slightly, adding to its ancient charm. A stone bridge over the moat leads through the 16th-century gatehouse into a delightful cobbled courtyard. The house forms three sides of the quadrangle with the fourth opening out on to the garden.

ELLESMERE PORT is a town with its feet rooted firmly in the present, its population expanding with the establishment of an oil refinery there. In the 19th century its development was founded on canals (right), as it formed the terminus of the Ellesmere Canal, later the Shropshire Union Canal, built in 1793. A museum at the docks includes more than 50 boats, as well as warehouses and workshops.

The great metal bowl of the **JODRELL BANK TELESCOPE**, 76 m (250 ft) in diameter, is one of the most remarkable modern features of the landscape, visible from all over the Cheshire Plain. Supported by 55 m (180 ft) metal towers, it can be rotated in all directions in search of radio signals. Erected in 1957, this was the first and largest of the telescopes built for Manchester University and it became famous in the 1960s for its connection with space programmes. Working models in the exhibition hall explain the telescope and there is also a planetarium with a 12 m (40 ft) projection dome.

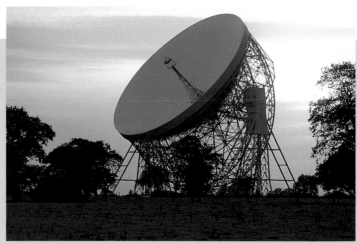

romantic was inexhaustible, began flocking to the lakes. John Ruskin, who moved to Brantwood, a house with magnificent views over Coniston Water, in 1871, was appalled by the influx of visitors, observing gloomily: 'You will soon have a tourist railway up Scafell and another up Helvellyn and another up Skiddaw, and then a connecting line all round.' The Lake District Association was formed in 1883, partly instigated by a close friend of Ruskin, Canon Rawnsley, and it was perhaps due to its early conservation aims that Ruskin's worst fears were never realized.

The largest and busiest of the lakes is Windermere, stretching 17 km (10½ miles) from north to south. Ullswater is scenically the most impressive, the oval Derwentwater is one of the prettiest and Wastwater the deepest and most mysterious.

The enormous popularity of the lakes tends to overshadow the rest of the region but there is plenty of interest here. The Cumbrian coast, with its deserted sandy beaches, is the place for bird-watchers, who can see dunlins, godwits, oystercatchers, sandpipers and wild geese. Across the estuary from Ravenglass is a large breeding colony of black-headed gulls. Over the border in Lancashire, Morecambe Bay claims one of the most beautiful bays in Britain, which is host to flocks of migratory birds in winter. The exhilarating air of Blackpool, that most rollicking of resorts, is said to be more like Guinness than champagne, while the more restrained Lytham St Anne's is known for its golf courses and quiet parks with colourful floral displays. Inland lies the lonely stretch of brown and green hills called the Forest of Bowland, filling most of the countryside between Clitheroe and Lancaster. Only one road runs through the Trough of Bowland, a wild pass through the steep fells.

Manchester was an important settlement in Roman times and today it is Britain's most handsome Victorian city, its buildings a monument to the prosperity brought by its status as the cradle of the cotton industry. Among the most notable are the Gothic-style Town Hall, with its 85 m (280 ft) tower, the John Rylands Library, designed by Basil Champneys, and the Free Trade Hall with its Palladian facade. ▷ **155**

LIVERPOOL, *first settled 2,000 years ago, prospered on trade with the West Indies, then grew rapidly in the 18th and 19th centuries to become Britain's largest port. The waterfront is lined by 11 km (7 miles) of docks, and the largest floating landing stage in the world is supported on 200 pontoons.*

*Behind the neo-renaissance dome of the docks office building rise the twin towers the **ROYAL LIVER BUILDING** (left) surmounted by the 'Liver' birds, surveying the Mersey and its shipping from a height of some 76 m (250 ft) above high-water mark. Though the birds have become the city's emblem their ancestry is a mystery, as they belong to no known species.*

*This is the only city in the country that can claim two cathedrals which were both built in this century. The enormous Anglican **LIVERPOOL CATHEDRAL**, chiefly the work of Sir Giles Gilbert Scott, was begun in 1904 and only finished in 1978. It is in the Gothic style, built of red sandstone, with floors of black and white marble. The **ROMAN CATHOLIC CATHEDRAL** is a complete contrast. Work was begun by Sir Edwin Lutyens in 1933 but the final building was designed by Sir Frederick Gibberd and was completed in 1965. It is circular, centring on the High Altar, with the roof reaching up to a coloured glass tower.*

*The **ALBERT DOCK**, opened in 1846 and closed in 1972, has been given a new lease of life with arcaded shops and attractive pubs. A riverside walk gives good views of modern Mersey traffic and an old warehouse houses the Merseyside Maritime Museum, with floating exhibits, models and craft demonstrations. The northern branch of the Tate Gallery displays a wide range of modern art.*

LANCASTER dates back to the time when the Romans established a camp on a bend in the River Lune. Later, the Normans built their castle here and the great keep, with its 3 m (10 ft) thick walls, still stands over the town. King John added to the castle and Elizabeth I strengthened its fortifications. It has served as a prison and a courthouse for hundreds of years. George Fox, founder of the Quakers, was once imprisoned here. There are grim reminders of past punishments: a cat-o'-nine-tails last used in 1915, and the clamp used to fasten a prisoner's hand while it was branded with a hot iron.

ST GEORGE'S QUAY (right), with its tall 18th-century warehouses, is a reminder of the time that Lancaster was a major port. The Old Custom House, with its elegant Ionic columns, was designed by Richard Gillow in 1764. It now houses a maritime museum, which includes the collector's office, restored to its 18th-century appearance, a display of port history and a fisherman's cottage of the 1920s.

ST MARY'S priory and parish church includes remnants of a Saxon building, but much of it dates from the 14th and 15th centuries. The carved woodwork of the 14th-century choir stalls, thought to have been brought from Furness Abbey, is outstanding.

Among those who were tried and executed at Lancaster Castle were the Lancashire **WITCHES** of 1612. Chief among them was Chattox, an ancient crone who robbed graveyards for the teeth of the dead, to use in her spells. Her greatest rival was 80-year-old Demdike, who claimed to have given her soul to the devil 50 years before. No one in the villages surrounding Pendle Hill, where the witches held their sabbats, doubted that they killed their enemies by bewitching them. Demdike died in prison but the remaining 10 women, charged with more than a dozen murders, were all hanged.

CASTLERIGG STONE CIRCLE (below) in Cumbria has a dramatic setting on a plateau, set in an amphitheatre of mountains. No one knows the purpose of this Bronze Age survival with its 38 stones, about 30 m (100 ft) in diameter, with 10 more stones set inside the circle, but there is a recognizable entrance between two large portal stones to the north. The poet John Keats, in **Hyperion**, described Castlerigg as 'a dismal cirque of Druid stones, upon a forlorn moor', but the site commands wonderful views of Skiddaw and Blencathra.

BORROWDALE (right) is one of the most beautiful of all the Lakeland valleys. Nowadays the fellsides are given over to sheep, but in the past rich deposits of graphite were found, and in 1566 the world's first pencil factory was opened in **KESWICK,** a few miles away. The workings are exhausted now and the factory, which houses a fascinating museum, imports lead for its pencils.

The region was the birthplace of pioneers whose work transformed the cotton industry: from Preston came Richard Arkwright, inventor of the spinning frame which made production more economical, while Bolton was the birthplace of Samuel Crompton, inventor of the spinning jenny. The Lewis Textile Museum in Blackburn tells the story of the heyday of cotton, with examples of the earliest machines. At Burnley the Weavers' Triangle, around the Leeds and Liverpool Canals, preserves weaving sheds, spinning mills and warehouses in a little corner of history.

The non-industrial history of the north-west can be traced through its many lovely houses. Turton Tower in Lancashire, mostly 16th century, was originally a peel tower dating from unsettled medieval times; so, too, was Levens Hall in Cumbria, near enough to the Scottish border to need defence against raids. Two of England's finest black and white houses are Little Moreton Hall in Cheshire, a moated manor house, and Bramall Hall, Greater Manchester, ▷ **161**

*Some of the most rewarding walking country of the Lake District is centred round **GRISEDALE** (left) and Patterdale. Climbers heading for the summit of **HELVELLYN**, the most popular of Cumbria's mountains, tramp across the Grisedale Fells before scrambling up Striding Edge, past the sparkling Red Tarn in its deep hollow and then up the scree slope to the 950 m (3,118 ft), summit. On the top are two memorials: one marks the landing of an aeroplane in 1926 and the other commemorates a dog which stayed for several weeks with its dead master in 1855.*

On the return, climbers can follow Glenridding Beck where it flows through dramatic ravines, past the old lead mines, or take the ridge south across Dollywagon Pikes to Grisedale Tarn, then back down to Patterdale.

*The mountains look out over the southern end of **ULLSWATER**, second in size only to Windermere. Summer steamers running between Glenridding and Pooley Bridge give the best views of the lake where Dorothy Wordsworth saw the 'fluttering and dancing' spring daffodils that inspired her brother's poem. Aira Force may not be the most spectacular of waterfalls but its setting, in a mossy, fern-edged cleft, is idyllic.*

Visitors to Hill Top Farm at Near Sawrey will recognize the house and the setting, for **BEATRICE POTTER** set six of her books here. The stoneflagged kitchen belonged to Mrs Tabitha Twitchit, down the hill is the farm where Jemima Puddle-Duck lived and the shop kept by Ginger and Pickles.

The author, who spent her youth in a large, gloomy London house, at the beck and call of domineering parents, spent holidays in the Lake District and fell in love with the countryside. She began sketching the plants and animals and eventually published *The Tale of Peter Rabbit*. Its success enabled her to buy the 17th-century farmhouse.

The tranquil beauty of many of the
Cumbrian hillsides remains undisturbed,
even in the tourist season (above).

    DOVE COTTAGE (right), at the east end of
the village of GRASMERE, was the home of
William Wordsworth for nine years. He
moved here with his sister Dorothy in 1799,
and the house is preserved as a shrine,
with the furniture and garden much as they
were in the poet's time. Thomas Gray
described the setting of Grasmere as 'one of
the sweetest landscapes that art ever
attempted to imitate'. The cluster of grey
stone farm buildings nesting quietly in a
wooded valley at the foot of HELM CRAG (far
right) cannot have changed very much since
Wordsworth wrote to Coleridge that from
the hill behind the cottage there was a view
'of the lake, the church, Helm Crag and
two thirds of the vale'. Wordsworth brought
his bride to Dove Cottage, but it was soon
too small for their growing family and eventually they moved to RYDAL MOUNT, south-
east of Grasmere, which was Wordsworth's
home for the last 37 years of his life.

St Oswald's Church in Grasmere has
preserved the ancient 'rush-bearing'
ceremony dating from medieval times when
rushes were scattered on the earth floor
and changed once a year. The whole village
takes part, making traditional designs from
rushes and flowers, to be borne into the
church by children who are rewarded with
pieces of gingerbread stamped with the name
of St Oswald. The gingerbread is produced
in a little shop by the lych gate, once
the village school. It is baked according to a
secret village recipe and exported all over
the world.

which dates from the 15th century, but has an arched timber roof over its banqueting hall that probably belonged to an earlier building. Also in Greater Manchester is Hall i' th' Wood, a half-timbered manor house begun 1483, with a stone wing added in 1591, which was once the home of Samuel Crompton, the inventor. The most visited house in the region is Tatton Park in Cheshire, completed in 1825, which is now owned by the National Trust. It was formerly the home of the Egerton family, who built up fascinating collections of furniture, pictures and silver. It stands in 22 ha (54 acres) of formal gardens laid out by Humphrey Repton and the 405 ha (1,000 acre) park contains a large mere, the haunt of wildfowl of many kinds.

Cheshire is particularly rich in delightful gardens. Norton Priory, the site of a medieval Augustinian foun-

*The **BUTTERMERE** valley on the western fringe of the district, has no less than three lakes, Buttermere, Crummock Water and Loweswater. The rounded peak of Little Dodd is seen here from Loweswater, which is ringed by woodlands, earning its name, which means 'leafy lake'. All three, which are very different in character, are owned by the National Trust. The scattered village of Loweswater has had a church since the 12th century though the present building dates from 1884.*

*   **SMARDALE VIADUCT** (above), near Kirkby Stephen, though a man-made intrusion into the landscape, is designed to blend with its natural setting.*

dation, has extensive woodland gardens laid out in the Georgian period, a pretty Victorian rock garden and a stream glade planted with azaleas. The rose gardens of Cholmondeley Castle, where honeysuckle and lavender mingle with an impressive variety of roses, date from the early l9th century, while Arley Hall has two huge herbaceous borders, 76 m (250 ft) long and backed by clipped yews, that were probably the first of their kind. It was already in existence in 1846, some 30 years before herbaceous borders were supposed to have been invented. Ness Gardens, on the Wirral, were planted in the late l9th century and have excellent collections of rhododendrons and azaleas, camellias and primulas, as well as views over the Dee estuary. □

*The **River Duddon** (above) flows through rocky defiles, below lowering crags and between banks carpeted with wild flowers in spring, on its way to its estuary near Broughton-in-Furness. The course of the river is at its most dramatic in Wallowbarrow Gorge where the water races between steep rock walls, thickly wooded with oak and beech, birch and elder.*

***Ulpha,** a lonely little village below the gorge, takes its name from the Scandinavian, meaning 'wolf hill'. Its church has interesting wall paintings and an altar made from a fruit tree.*

LINGMOOR FELL (below) rises over 457 m (1,500 ft), between Great Langdale and Little Langdale, its slopes shadowing the deep Blea Tarn, with clumps of pines and rhododendrons on its shores, described by Wordsworth as 'so lonesome and so perfectly secure'.

GREAT LANGDALE is one of the most popular tourist centres in the Lake District, offering exciting walks and climbs. One of the easiest walks takes in Dungeon Ghyll Force, where the water plunges through a chasm, then continues to the silent mountain lake of Stickle Tarn, below the 152 m (500 ft) rock slab of Pavey Ark.

The more adventurous can continue to the top of the **LANGDALE PIKES**, taking in Harrison Stickle, Loft Craig and Pike of Stickle. Just below the summit of Pike of Stickle is a neolithic stone axe 'factory', where ancient man fashioned his tools.

THE NORTH-WEST

HIGH STREET (right) is an old Roman road built across the high moorland at a time when routes through the valleys might have brought the Roman legions into conflict with hostile local tribes. It ran from Brougham, near Penrith, to Ambleside and still makes an exhilarating walk, with springy turf underfoot and some splendid views. The whole area is littered with standing stones, cairns and stone circles, all dating back thousands of years, their original purpose lost in antiquity.

To the east lies HAWESWATER, an isolated lake enlarged into a reservoir by flooding the valley of Mardale. The ruins of the village church can still be seen below the water and local people insist that they hear the bells ringing on wild nights.

SHAP ABBEY, in a quiet valley below High Street, was founded in the 12th century and though only the tower still stands, the original buildings can be identified from the remaining stones. A short walk leads to the little 16th-century chapel at Keld.

MARTINDALE, towards Ullswater, has a centuries-old deer forest and a chapel dating from 1633, with an ancient yew tree that provided the wood for the bows of local archers who fought at Flodden.

POOLEY BRIDGE stands at the northern end of High Street and the northern tip of Ullswater. Its name means 'pool by the hill'; it has lost its pool but kept its bridge. In the hills beyond is Dacre, its 14th-century peel tower a reminder of turbulent times, when Scots raids across the border were frequent. The Venerable Bede records a monastery at Dacre in AD 731, and it was probably there that King Athelstan of England met with the Scots to sign a treaty in AD 926.

WILD CALEDONIA

*The rugged independence
of the Scottish spirit is mirrored
in its wild mountains and
dark, secret glens, its jagged
seascape, gnawed by Atlantic
rollers, and its untouched
tracts of wilderness, the last
refuge for many rare species.
Offshore lie a generous
scattering of lonely, lovely
islands, many inhabited
only by birds.*

*The waters of Loch Ness, shadowed by the surrounding
hills, seem a natural hiding place for some prehistoric
monster. The best place for a sighting of the legendary
'Nessie' is supposed to be from the ruins of Castle
Urquhart, on a bluff above the loch.*

SCOTLAND

The Scots insist that, once across the border from England, the very air smells purer and clearer. The pride of the Scots in all things Scottish, from scenery to football teams, has always been one of their outstanding characteristics. Though in modern times Scotland's history has been that of the rest of Britain, they had their own Parliament until 1707 and still retain their own legal system, Church and even their own banknotes. They retain a reputation for being independent and outspoken, determined and courageous, thrifty and hard-headed, but with an underlying streak of romanticism.

The Border Country, with its gentle valleys and sheep-dotted hills, looks peaceful enough now, but its past has been savage and turbulent. Even the towns have a stern heritage: Jedburgh's justices were well known for executing the accused first and proceeding to trial afterwards, and Galashiels keeps its motto 'Sour Plums', which commemorates the 14th-century slaughter of a party of English intruders who were suffering from the effects of eating wild plums. The impressive ruins of the medieval abbeys of Melrose, Dryburgh, Kelso and Jedburgh bear witness to centuries of turmoil. They were built in the 12th century, in a period of political stability when David I aimed to 'civilize' the country along Norman-English lines. However, there was to be no tranquillity for the great ecclesiastical buildings; they stood in the path of later English invasions and frontier disputes and were repeatedly sacked and burned until they were finally destroyed in the 16th century.

Sir Walter Scott, born in Edinburgh but spending most of his life at Abbotsford House, a mansion in Scottish Baronial style near Melrose, used the stirring tales of Scottish history and legends in his novels, painting romantic word pictures of his native countryside: Victorian tourists flocked to the Trossachs after reading his poem **The Lady of the Lake,** and one of his novels immortalized the rough farmers and heather-covered hillsides of the Braes of Balquhidder, the native heath of his hero Rob Roy. The other towering figure of Scottish literature is Robert Burns, the bard who speaks for the ordinary Scot. Few poets have such an important place in the hearts of a nation as Burns, who wrote so lyrically about the places he loved — 'bonnie Doon', 'sweet

168

KIRKCUDBRIGHT takes its name from the 'Church of Cuthbert', an old church where the remains of the saint once rested. The pretty little port on the River Dee is the capital of old Stewartry — a term meaning crown property administered by a steward. In the late 19th century it became the adopted home of painters, sculptors and craftsmen and it still has a vigorous art colony.

At the harbour stands McLellan's Castle, a turreted mansion built in 1582 by the Provost Sir Thomas McLellan, with stones from the old friary. It has been a ruin since the 18th century. Greyfriars Church incorporates fragments of the 13th-century friary church and preserves McLellan's tomb. The town also has a mercat (market) cross dating from 1610.

DUNDRENNAN ABBEY, a few kilometres away, was founded in 1142 by David I and Fergus, Lord of Galloway. It was here that Mary, Queen of Scots, spent her last night in Scotland in 1568. She then made her way to England, to ask her cousin, Queen Elizabeth, for sanctuary, but found herself imprisoned instead – now only the ruins of the once prosperous abbey remain.

Afton', the 'brigs of Ayr' — that any journey through the south-west seems like a pilgrimage.

The English love affair with the Highlands and Islands of Scotland began when Queen Victoria and her husband Prince Albert bought Balmoral as their summer home in 1848. Albert designed a special 'Balmoral' tartan, which was liberally used in carpets, curtains and upholstery. Each holiday saw them becoming determinedly more Scottish, and the aristocracy and monied

SCOTT'S VIEW (left) looks out from a hill-top in Scott's beloved Borderland, across Old Melrose, the crescent bends of the River Tweed and the Eildon Hills. The spot was so closely associated with Sir Walter Scott that his funeral procession halted here on the way to his burial at Dryburgh Abbey.

*The **EILDON HILLS** are rich in history and legend: Sir Walter Scott said: 'I can stand on the Eildon Hills and point out forty-three places famous in war and verse.' He related the legend of Michael Scott, the Border wizard, who had to find work for a clansman and set him to split the single hill of Eildon into the present three peaks, then to spin endless ropes of sand at the mouth of the Tweed. It was here that Thomas the Rhymer met with the Queen of Elfland and received the gift of poetic prophecy. Beneath the hills, King Arthur and his knights are said to be sleeping, destined to wake one day.*

***LINLITHGOW PALACE** (far left) is another of the many romantic spots of the Lowland and Border region, its ruined, fire-stained stones standing on a promontory beside the town loch. There was a royal residence here as early as the 12th century but the present palace was begun in 1425, in the time of James I. The Chapel and Great Hall, with its enormous fireplace, are both 15th century and the richly carved fountain in the quadrangle was added by James V.*

James V was born in the palace in 1512 and his daughter Mary, Queen of Scots, in 1542. Charles I, who considered making Linlithgow the capital of Scotland, was the last king to sleep within the walls, in 1633, and the last Scottish parliament met here in 1646.

classes followed them in large numbers, acquiring shooting lodges and tramping the grouse moors. The north of Scotland, with its great stretches of uninhabited countryside, its serrated granite peaks, its hillsides clad in orange bracken and purple heather, its fjord-like inlets and mirror-smooth lochs, has exercised an enormous fascination ever since.

Before the 18th century, when military roads were built in the Highlands in the days of the ▷ **177**

EDINBURGH CASTLE (right), *clinging to its volcanic ledge high above the city, has been a fortress from the earliest times. It was in 1076 that Malcolm III's wife Margaret, later to become St Margaret, built the simple little chapel that is the oldest surviving part of the castle.*

In the royal apartments is the room where Mary, Queen of Scots, gave birth to her son, the future James VI of Scotland and I of England. Nearby is the Crown Chamber, containing the Honours of Scotland: the crown, sceptre and sword of state.

From the castle, the Royal Mile slopes down through the Old Town to the small but proud Palace of Holyrood House, a royal residence since the time of James IV. The elegant 'New Town' is an area of generous squares and handsome Georgian houses, majestically designed in the late 18th century.

*Below this well-planned area, in a ravine, is *DEAN VILLAGE* (below), once a busy mill centre, now a picturesque jumble of buildings beside the Water of Leith.*

TOBERMORY (left), the chief town on the island of Mull, takes its name from the Gaelic for 'Well of Mary'. In 1788 the British Fisheries Society planned and developed the little town as a fishing port, but after the herring shoals deserted the bay the population dropped dramatically. Recently it has become popular as a yachting centre and a holiday base for exploring the island.

At the bottom of the bay lies the Spanish galleon **Florida**, a survivor of the Armada which took shelter there in 1588. When the ship tried to leave without paying for stores supplied by the town, a clansman of the Macleans was sent aboard to collect the money. He was imprisoned by the Spaniards but managed to escape and blew up the magazine, sinking the ship. Divers still hunt for treasure but the vessel has kept most of its secrets.

One of the most interesting walks from the village leads to **AROS CASTLE**, a 13th-century ruin set on a promontory in Salen Bay, once a stronghold of the Lords of the Isles, now a peaceful spot with a good show of rhododendrons. Another popular walk runs around the bay to the lighthouse at Rubha-nan-Gall and Bloody Bay, the scene of a great sea battle between John, Lord of the Isles, and his son in 1439.

In the remote farmhouse of **BARNHILL**, on the Hebridean island of Jura, George Orwell wrote his novel *1984*, a powerful warning of what could happen if the state were given too much power over individuals. He fell in love with the isolation of the spot when visiting the island and insisted on renting the house, though it had been empty for a long time and was without electricity or telephone. He lived there from 1946 to 1949, refusing to leave before the book was finished, though his health deteriorated badly in the cold and damp. He finally left the island for hospital and died of tuberculosis in January 1950.

Jacobite rebellions, the English believed that the Scots of the north were fearsome barbarians. The whole system of Scottish society, with its strong reliance on clans, seemed strange and primitive. Though the Gaelic word *clann* simply means 'family', the clansmen swore allegiance to a chief, who had the power of life and death over his followers. Rivalries between clans often led to bloody battles and massacres.

Highland gatherings, once organized by clan chiefs as a method of picking the strongest fighting men, have proliferated, spreading far beyond the Highlands. Something like 100 are held each year with competitors and entertainers in full regalia. For tourists they are the epitome of Scotland, with twirling kilts, folk dancing, day-long bagpipe music and burly Scots putting the

In the remote Highlands, amid some of the country's most beautiful mountain and glen scenery lie LOCH DUICH and GLEN SHIEL (left), near the journey's end on one of the Roads to the Isles travelled by Dr Johnson and Boswell in 1773. EILEAN DONAN CASTLE (above), standing where Loch Duich meets Lochs Long and Alsh, is one of the most photographed and filmed of Highland castles. Built in 1220 to guard against Viking attack, it was occupied in 1719 by Spanish troops backing the Jacobite rebellion: three English frigates sailed up Loch Alsh and bombarded it. It was rebuilt early this century.

LOCH LEVEN (above), a slender finger of sea, reaches into the western Highlands from Loch Linnhe, its shores offering magnificent walking and climbing country.

At **BALLACHULISH**, at the mouth of the loch on the southern shore, the old ferry crossing used by travellers bound for Fort William was replaced by a bridge in the 1970s. Near the bridge is a cairn built for James of the Glens, tried and hanged by the Campbells for the murder of one of their number in 1755; Robert Louis Stevenson used the story in **Kidnapped**.

KINLOCHLEVEN stands at the head of the loch, its busy aluminium works contrasting with the peace and beauty of the loch. A path leads over the Devil's Staircase, an old military road, to the Pass of Glencoe.

shot, throwing the hammer, wrestling and racing. One of the favourite events, caber tossing, is supposed to have originated in the throwing of felled trees into the middle of the river. When telegraphic communications first came to the north, many a telegraph pole went missing; they were just the right size for caber tossing!

Despite its often inhospitable climate, the Highlands have always been associated with outdoor pursuits, both winter and summer. Scotland's ski resorts can rival those of Europe for scenery and facilities if not for sunshine. Every August the landed gentry, plus large numbers of rich businessmen, gather on the Highland grouse moors for the 'Glorious Twelfth'. Fishermen find a rich haul in the salmon rivers, and excellent fishing can be found in freshwater lochs and streams.

Where there are few people, spacious moors and extensive forests, wildlife can flourish undisturbed. Pine martens, almost killed off in the 19th century, are once more found in the remote north. Golden eagles soar high in the mountains and buzzards are often seen, though the peregrine falcon is a rare sight. Ospreys, killed in Britain in the early part of the century because they competed so successfully with the fishermen for trout, began to return to the protected habitats of the reserves in the 1950s.

On the Orkneys and Shetlands, the number of people seems insignificant beside the vast flocks of birds that jostle for every inch of space on the cliffs and stark rocks: guillemots, kittiwakes, Arctic terns, auks, storm petrels, gulls and skuas, which can be aggressive towards humans in the breeding season. There are waders and wheatears, shearwaters, snowy owls and puffins, which arrive in May and can number around 300,000.□

RED DEER have doubled in number over the past three decades and deer stalking is a popular pursuit of the wealthy, but those who simply want to admire the grace of these animals can see them roaming the high moorlands in summer and the wooded glens in winter. Red deer are the largest wild animals native to Britain, they stand 1.2 m (4 ft) high at the shoulder.

GLENCOE, where Highland scenery is at its awe-inspiring best, is the most famous — or infamous of all Scottish glens. It is known as the 'Glen of Weeping', for this was the scene of a terrible massacre of the Macdonalds by the Campbells.

After the failure of the Jacobite cause, the chiefs of the Highland clans were required to sign an oath of allegiance to William III by 1 January 1692. Various accidental delays meant that the Glencoe chief signed the oath five days late and the government, with the connivance of the Campbells, decided to make an example of the clan.

For 12 days a company of Campbell soldiers were billeted in the glen, on the pretext that there was no room for them in the nearest town, and they were hospitably received. In the early hours of 13 February 1692 the sign for the massacre to begin was given from SIGNAL ROCK, on the north side of the River Coe. The orders were for the whole clan to be slaughtered and said that the 'manner of execution must be sure, secret and effectual'. Some 40 of the 200 clan members died, including women and babies; the rest were able to escape because a blizzard prevented soldiers from sealing off the area. A Celtic cross stands in 'memory of MacIain, Chief of Glencoe, who fell with his people in the massacre of Glencoe'

At the head of the glen is a rock terrace called THE STUDY (from an old Scots word meaning 'anvil'), commanding excellent views of the hills known as the Three Sisters. On the westernmost hill is the deep cleft of Ossian's Cave where, according to legend, the 3rd-century Gaelic hero was born.

SCOTLAND

The **RIVER SPEY** (right) is Scotland's second longest river, rising as a modest stream on the hills above Loch Laggan, then reaching its true splendour as it runs between the Cairngorms and the Monadhliaths, flowing through some of Scotland's most spectacular mountain scenery.

AVIEMORE is the most popular of the Spey Valley resorts, with the multi-million-pound complex providing a huge range of indoor and outdoor recreation facilities. Nearby is the **GLEN MORE FOREST PARK**, covering large areas of pine forest surrounding Loch Morlich, and reindeer, introduced from Lapland in 1952, live on the higher slopes.

The **CAIRNGORMS**, with six summits over 1,220 m (4,000 ft), is Britain's highest mountain mass. On Cairngorm itself, 1,245 m (4,084 ft) high, it is sometimes possible to ski in summertime. The majestic peaks are often used by climbers training for Himalayan expeditions; though they are at a comparatively low altitude, the conditions and complexity of the climbs are reminiscent of those encountered in Kashmir and Nepal.

The Spey is a major salmon river and many salmon make their way to spawning grounds in streams below the mountains, as much as 160 km (100 miles) from the mouth of the river. At Tugnet, on Spey Bay, an ice house built in 1860 has been converted into a museum to tell the story of the river and its fish.

Rough-hewn headstones mark the communal graves of those who fell in the battle of **CULLODEN**; grouped according to their clans, they form a semi-circle opposite a memorial cairn dating from 1881. The Highland clans had rallied to the support of Charles Edward Stuart, the Young Pretender, when he arrived from France in 1745. His period of glory was brief and the Jacobite cause was finally destroyed in April 1746 at Culloden. The Prince's troops were vastly outnumbered; the battle lasted only 40 minutes, but left 1,000 Jacobites dead.

The **ISLAND OF LEWIS** (left) belongs to the kite-shaped chain of islands of the Outer Hebrides, their coasts battered by Atlantic waves, their rolling moorlands windswept and desolate. Stornaway is the only town of any size and the rest of the islanders are scattered in small villages around the coast.

The STANDING STONES OF CALLANISH on the west coast of Lewis, indicate that primitive man lived here over 4,000 years ago. One large cairn is encircled by thirteen monoliths and rows of stones radiate from the circle.

The tiny crofts that used to characterize the islands still exist, but it is becoming harder to eke out a subsistence living from crofting alone. The old-style 'black houses', with the family's living area, byre and barn all together under one roof, have now been converted, or turned into museums.

On both Lewis and the adjoining island of **HARRIS**, (above) pure Scottish wool is still handwoven by the islanders in their homes, to produce the famous Harris tweed. Competition from man-made fibres have meant that later production processes are carried out in the mills of Stornaway.

LAND OF SAINTS AND SCHOLARS

This is a land where the pace is gentle, change comes slowly and memories are long. The countryside itself is tranquil, with rolling brown turf, fertile green pastureland and twinkling lakes. The gentle light gives a gentle focus and brings out the soft greens and blues of the fields and mountains.

The little resort of Gortahork, the centre of Donegal's Gaelic-speaking area, is well placed for those who want to enjoy the wild seascapes and coloured cliffs backing into craggy granite mountains that are the pride of this quiet county.

The beauties of Ireland have been immortalized in song and story, so it comes as something of a surprise to find that the famous names — the Mountains of Mourne, the Isle of Innisfree, Galway Bay, the lakes of Connemara really exist, and are just as lovely as the songs and poems that extol them. The less trumpeted areas have much to offer too: the haunting loveliness of the glens of Antrim, the sylvan valleys of Wicklow, the stark grandeur of the cliffs of Kerry, its sea-carved promontories bright with wild flowers, the castle country of County Cork.

Horse-drawn caravans and jaunting cars still seen the most suitable method of travel along quiet roads where beech trees touch branches overhead and walls and hedges are covered with a profusion of fuchsias and roses. It rains frequently but, unlike the English, the Irish seldom bother to mention it. Rain is an integral part of the scene; it brings the rich green colour and the riot of flowers, both in gardens and blooming wild along the roadside.

*The **ANTRIM COAST** (left) has a dramatic beauty, with the limestone cliffs near the seaside resort of Portrush carved into jagged rocks, arches and caves. The town stands on the promontory of Ramore Head, with fine stretches of beach on either side.*

***DUNLUCE CASTLE** (above) clings to the edge of a rocky crag, approached by a wooden bridge which replaced the old drawbridge. Built in the 13th century, it was a stronghold of the MacDonnells, Lords of the Isles, in the 16th century. In 1639 part of the cliff gave way and the kitchens and eight servants fell into the sea. Later, the Earls of Antrim moved away, and the rest of the castle fell into decay, but two towers, the gatehouse and the ruins of the great hall remain. Visitors can take a boat to the cave beneath the castle, which once provided a secret entrance from the sea.*

No one knows when, or in what numbers, the Celts arrived from Central Europe, but by 300 BC they were firmly established in Ireland. Though the Romans conquered Britain they never bothered to cross the Irish Sea, so Ireland was left to develop in its own way. When St Patrick established his church in Armagh, Ulster, in AD 440 and set about converting the Irish to Christianity, the country became known as the 'Island of Saints and Scholars' and the great monasteries like Glendalough were renowned as centres of learning. In the 6th and 7th centuries, Irish monks set out to spread the faith to other lands: Columba to Scotland, Brendan perhaps to America, Columbanus to France and Italy, Aidan to England. When the Viking raiders arrived, the monasteries became prime targets because of the valuables housed there. Many were left in ruins but it is still impossible to travel far in this country without finding the remains of chapels, holy places and decorated crosses, and the museums house magnificent illuminated manuscripts. Clonmacnois, County Offaly, founded in AD 548 by St Ciaran, was once a great monastic city and medieval university. It has a cathedral, eight churches and some splendid carved grave slabs. Elaborately carved 10th-century High Crosses stand at Monasterboice, Count Louth, while nearby is the ruined Mellifont, the country's first Cistercian abbey, founded in 1140. The world's finest illuminated manuscript, the **Book of Kells**, was produced in the 8th century in County Meath; Kells still has a well preserved medieval Round Tower and five High Crosses.

The tradition of travelling bards, who told heroic stories, lasted until 200 years ago in Ireland, long after it had died out elsewhere. The gift of 'blarney' is especially Irish and every boatman and jaunting-car driver entertains tourists with a rich blend of history and legend. St Patrick, they say, was the son of a Roman officer, kidnapped from his home in England, who spent his youth as a shepherd on the Antrim hills. On Croagh Patrick, in County Mayo, he performed a miracle by banishing all the snakes from Ireland. Robert the Bruce took refuge on Rathlin Island, County Antrim, when he fled from the English in 1306, and any local will point out the cave where he watched a spider patiently trying to reach the roof on a slender thread and was inspired to return to Scotand to 'try, try, try again'. Archaeologists may have identified the ancient stone enclosures of County Sligo as forts but the villagers have always called them 'royalties', the places where the Little People hold their most important ceremonies.

Everyday Irish speech is so lilting and mellifluous that it seems natural for the country to have produced so many great writers. Nobel Prize-winning poet William Butler Yeats made extensive use of Gaelic

MOUNT STEWART (above right) in County Down, the seat of the Marquess of Londonderry, was the birthplace of Lord Castlereagh, England's foreign secretary during the Napleonic wars. He succeeded to the title of Marquess in 1821, the year before he committed suicide.

The present house dates from the first half of the 19th century. The interior was furnished and decorated by the 7th Marchioness of Londonderry when her husband took over in 1915. She was also responsible for the glorious profusion of plants that have made the gardens famous. Though she originally planned them on

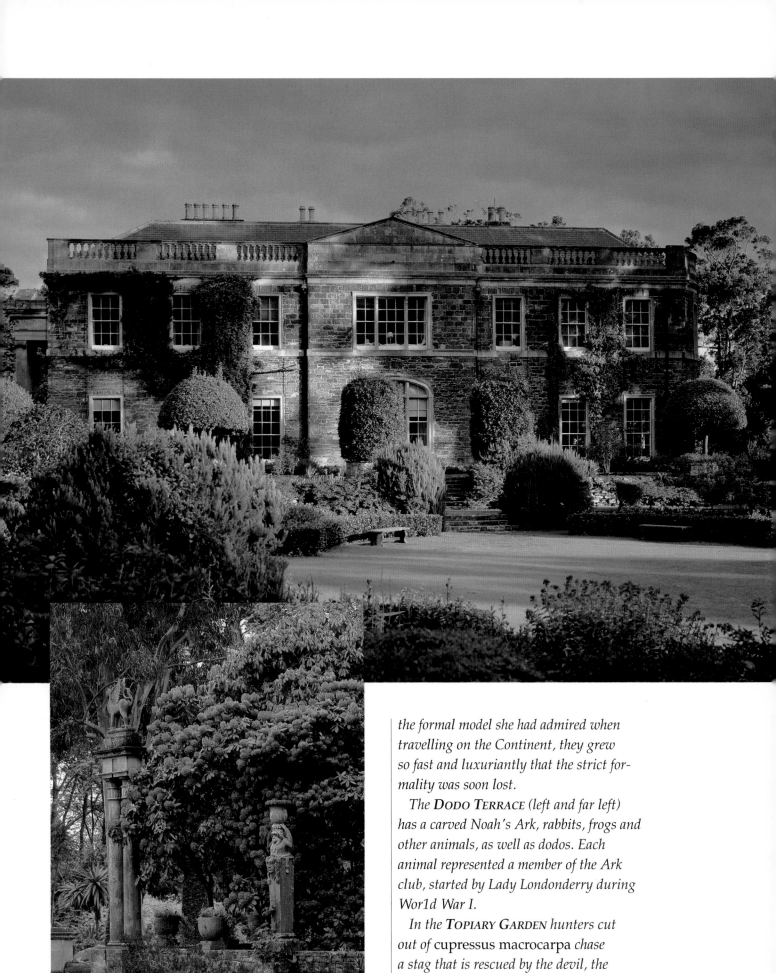

the formal model she had admired when
travelling on the Continent, they grew
so fast and luxuriantly that the strict for-
mality was soon lost.

The **DODO TERRACE** (left and far left)
has a carved Noah's Ark, rabbits, frogs and
other animals, as well as dodos. Each
animal represented a member of the Ark
club, started by Lady Londonderry during
World War I.

In the **TOPIARY GARDEN** hunters cut
out of cupressus macrocarpa chase
a stag that is rescued by the devil, the
figures representing members of Lady
Londonderry's family.

191

legends in his poetry, and the wild beauty of the Aran Islands was the inspiration for J.M. Synge. George Bernard Shaw was the giant of the British theatre for over 50 years, though the sharp wit of fellow-Dubliner Oscar Wilde has proved more popular with modern audiences. More recently, Edna O'Brien, Frank O'Connor and Sean O'Faolain have drawn on the scenes and settings of Ireland for their novels.

Colourful folk festivals are an integral part of local life. In August the fishing fleet, decked with colourful flags, assembles in Galway Bay for the ceremonial Blessing of the Sea, and in September the Oyster Festival there goes on for three days and nights, with the queen of the festivities presenting the first oyster of the season to the Mayor. The Harp Festival, which originated in County Longford in the 18th century, was revived in the early 1980s, but Kerry's Puck Fair has origins that are lost in history. Some maintain that the festival, which crowns a horned billy goat as king, commemorates the time when a herd of goats took fright and gave warning of an English attack, but it is more likely to have its roots in pagan fertility rituals.

Along with pride in the past, pride in craftmanship has been passed down through the generations, and traditional Irish occupations have received a boost from tourism. The birthplace of the world-famous Irish linen was Lisburn in County Antrim, where it was started in 1698 by Louis Crommelin, with Huguenots who fled from France in the reign of Louis XIV. Though there are factories turning out synthetic materials with the 'linen look', the genuine article is still made. At one time the art of cut crystal had almost died out but now it is flourishing again. The purest and most elaborate crystal comes from Waterford, but Tyrone crystal, from Northern Ireland, has also become famous. The fine china of Belleek, County Fermanagh, has been made since 1857, when local clay deposits were found. Its delicate lustre 'baskets' look as though they were woven from lace. The distinctive patterns of the thick, hand-knitted Aran sweaters — trellis, sea-horse, etc. — are the 'family' stitch patterns worn by Aran fishermen for generations. All too often, in the past, they were the means by which women identified their ▷ 198

BEN BULBEN (left) *raises its flat limestone head at the western end of the Dartry mountains in County Sligo and its slopes are rich in legend. It was here that the Gaelic hero Finn MacCool finally managed to kill his rival Diarmid, who had eloped with his beloved Grainne the night before he was to have married her.*

Below the mountain is the town of DRUMCLIFF, *where an elaborately carved High Cross marks the site of an ancient monastery, said to have been founded by St Columba after the 'battle of the books'. This was fought between the followers of Columba and those of Finian, who claimed that Columba had made an unauthorised copy of his psalter. Three thousand men died, and as a penance Columba built the monastery before leaving to convert the heathen in Scotland.*

LISSADELL HOUSE, *along the bay, is a lovely house built in the classical style in the 1830s for Sir Robert Gore-Booth. His granddaughters both achieved fame: Eva Gore-Booth as a poet and Constance, who became Countess Markievicz, as the first woman elected to the British House of Commons, though she preferred to take her seat in the Dail Eireann in Dublin instead. Yeats wrote of them as 'both beautiful, one a gazelle' and Sarah Purser's portrait of them can be seen in Lissadell House.*

William Butler **YEATS** is buried in the churchyard at Drumcliff, where his grandfather had been vicar. He had asked to be buried 'Under bare Ben Bulben's head' and wrote his own epitaph. Yeats used many of the traditions and legends of County Sligo in his work and Galway, too, has many reminders of the poet. Near Gort, where the home of Lady (Augusta) Gregory once stood, is a beech tree carved with his initials and those of other Irish writers, and Thoor Ballylee, the house where he lived for 12 years, is a museum.

The **ARAN ISLANDS**, *part of a limestone outcrop that forms a barrier across the approaches to Galway Bay, were in the past remote and inaccessible, so that the inhabitants have retained much of their traditional way of life and the islands themselves have kept their unspoilt charm.*

Heavy seas smash against the high cliffs of **INISHMORE** *(right), the 'Great Island', which has interesting antiquities, chief among them the prehistoric fort of Dun Aengus. Perched 91 m (300 ft) above the sea, it forms a great semicircle, with three lines of ramparts.*

The land is barren and stony, with few trees, and the islanders have had to create their own soil from sand and seaweed, clearing away the loose rocks by hand and using them to create the maze of drystone walls that divide the fields where cattle graze and basic crops grow. The smallest and prettiest of the islands is Inisheer. Another is Inishmaan, the setting for J.M. Synge's **Riders to the Sea.**

The **CLIFFS OF MOHER** (*far right*) *rise over 198 m (650 ft) above the Atlantic on the coast of County Clare, the crashing waves gnawing at the feet of the sheer headlands, sending up plumes of spray. Though the l9th-century tower built as a tea house by the MP Cornelius O'Brien does nothing to enhance the view on land, it makes a splendid lookout for one of Ireland's most dramatic seascapes.*

LISDOONVARNA, a short way inland, has been well known as a spa since the 18th century: its sulphur and chalybeate springs help in the treatment of rheumatism. It also has a reputation as a match-making centre, dating from the time when bachelor farmers began gathering there after harvest, on the lookout for eligible young ladies.

The resort makes a good centre for exploring THE BURREN, an extraordinary grey limestone plateau. Cromwell's soldiers found it a miserable place, with 'neither water enough to drown a man, nor a tree to hang him, nor soil enough to bury him'. However, this barren desert look is deceptive, for every crack in the rock nurtures myriad small plants and flowers including gentians, primroses, cinquefoil and wild orchids.

In prehistoric times the Burren must have seemed less inhospitable, for it is scattered

with cairns, ring-forts and tombs. At POULNABRONE is a fine portal dolmen (left), where the bones of 20 people were found, together with pottery and other artefacts dating back around 4,500 years. The rock is riddled with caves and potholes; the Aillwee Cave has stalactites, stalacmites and an underground river and Ireland's longest cave, the POUL-AN-IONAIN complex, extends for 11 km (7 miles). The bones of reindeer, elk, bear and, most surprising of all, African wild cat, have been found inside.

The area has many picturesque towers and castles, including the old circular tower inside a small bawn, or fortified enclosure, at DOONAGORE (above) and the five storey round tower on a square base at Newtown.

LEAMANEAGH CASTLE is an impressive ruin, with a 15th-century tower and the remains of a 17th-century mansion. It was once a stronghold of the powerful O'Briens. In the 17th century it was owned by Conor O'Brien, was killed in battle by Cromwell's troops. His widow straightaway offered to marry any Cromwellian soldier, in order to keep possession of her home.

The nearby village of KILFENORA has a display centre covering the botany and geology of the Burren, as well as the little l2th-century cathedral of St Fachan and a superbly carved High Cross.

drowned menfolk; now they make quality souvenirs.

The ancient provinces of Leinster, Munster and Connaught were once ruled by great kings; now they are part of the Republic of Ireland, along with the three counties of Donegal, Monaghan and Cavan, historically part of Ulster. When the treaty of 1921 brought the fighting between England and Ireland to a close and partitioned the country, the six northern counties – Derry, Tyrone, Fermanagh, Armagh, Down and Antrim – chose to remain part of the United Kingdom.

Dublin, the capital of the Republic, has a relaxed atmosphere and a slightly faded elegance that many find captivating. It seems to have grown organically and town planning came too late to do anything but complicate its convoluted street pattern. Belfast, the chief city of the north, is more formal and modern-looking, its streets planned on a grid system in the late 18th century, its proudest buildings Victorian. It lacks the dreamy charm of Dublin and is more down-to-earth.

LOUGH LEANE (below) is the largest of the celebrated lakes of Killarney, romantically situated below MacGillycuddy's Reeks, Ireland's highest group of mountains. The 2,024 ha (5,000 acre) lake is dotted with more than 30 little islands, one of the most attractive of them being Innisfallen, which has the ruins of a 7th-century abbey.

Along the eastern bank lies the Muckross estate, now the Bourne-Vincent Memorial Park, with its splendid collection of bamboos, ferns, azaleas and hydrangeas. Most of the ruins of Muckross Abbey date from the 15th century, though it was founded in 1340. It has the tombs of several important Kerry families and delightful cloisters surrounding an old yew tree. Muckross House, built in Tudor style in 1843, has a folk museum and craft shops.

The **GAP OF DUNLOE**, a narrow, rocky defile through the mountains, was formed by glaciers, though legend says that the mighty Finn MacCool created it with a blow of his sword. Visitors travel through on horseback or by pony and trap, and from the head of the gap there is a breathtaking view of the Upper Lake, its shores covered with arbutus and royal fern, and the Black Valley, stretching away into the heart of the MacGillycuddy Reeks. The return journey to Killarney can be made by boat, down the modest 'rapids' by Dinis Island to the Middle, or Muckross Lake.

The boat journey usually ends at **ROSS CASTLE**, back on Lough Leane. The 15th-century stronghold was the last place in Munster to be taken by Cromwell's army in 1652.

LITTLE SKELLIG (above) is one of several jagged pinnacles rising from the fierce sea off the coast of Kerry. Its steep 134 m (440 ft) rock has a breeding colony of about 18,000 gannets, a fascinating sight as they plunge from a great height into the waves in search of fish. Apart from the gannets, there are plentiful puffins, shearwaters and petrels.

Great Skellig, or Skellig Michael, has a well-preserved 7th-century monastery with six drystone 'beehive' huts, two oratories and two primitive crosses, all neatly bounded by a protective wall. This was once a place of pilgrimage, with pilgrims scrambling to the very top of the rock to make their penance. It is only possible to approach the islands by boat when the sea is sufficiently calm, which may mean waiting for several weeks.

ST FINBARR'S CATHEDRAL (left) is an extraordinary Gothic edifice, its 40 m (131 ft) centre spire rearing far above the surrounding buildings in the city of Cork. The present Church of Ireland Cathedral replaced a Georgian building which was pulled down in 1864. A competition held to decide on an architect for its replacement was won by William Burges of London.

GLANNORE LAKE (left), with its peaceful wooded islands, is one of the scenic views from the Healy Pass, the high road winding across the Caha Mountains. There are also impressive views out over the Kenmare river and MacGillycuddy's Reeks. The pass was begun as a famine relief project but only completed in 1928 under the auspices of Tim Healy, the first governor-general of the Free State.

BEARA is the quietest and least frequented of the lovely west coast peninsulas but the drive is delightful, starting from Kenmare, the little market town founded in 1670, and running along the north coast past the wooded gardens of Derreen House with their profusion of rhododendrons, azaleas and New Zealand tree ferns before crossing the border between County Cork and County Kerry. At Eyeries stands the tallest ogham stone in Ireland, over 5 m (15 ft) high. These stones take their name from Ogmios, the Celtic god of writing and are memorials marked with a 4th-century adaptation of the Latin alphabet.

DUNBOY CASTLE, now roofless, was the scene of a heroic defence by a Spanish-Irish garrison against the siege by English forces in 1602. Its commander almost succeeded in blowing up the fortress but the English broke in just in time to stop him and put the survivors to death.

The local village, CASTLETOWN BEARHAVEN, the largest on the peninsula, faces the quiet waters of Bantry Bay, and offshore is Bear Island, a naval base for the British Atlantic fleet until 1937. Nearby Allihies was a copper-mining centre in the 19th century and provided the background for Daphne du Maurier's novel **Hungry Hill**, named after the highest of the Caha mountains, rising to 684 m (2,244 ft).

The city owes its existence to St Finbarr, who founded a monastery on the south side of the main channel of the River Lee in about the 6th century. The city expanded when Danish invaders settled here and by the 12th century it was the capital of the kingdom of South Munster. It is now the third largest city in Ireland, prosperous and lively, a busy seaport and manufacturing centre.

GLENDALOUGH (left), the 'valley of two lakes' in County Wicklow, was the serene and beautiful setting chosen by St Kevin, who established a simple hermitage here in the 6th century. The monastic settlement that followed became a renowned seat of learning and though it was raided by the Danes, it survived until the 15th century. The 33 m (108 ft) Round Tower is well preserved, its top reconstructed with the original stones, and there are also the remains of several churches and crosses and a 9th-century cathedral.

St Kevin's Kitchen is a two storey oratory with a steep, pitched stone roof, its belfry a little round tower. A hollowed-out rock near the stream is the Deer Stone, where a white doe is supposed to have come regularly to be milked by St Kevin, while high on the bank of the upper lake is a rock shelf known as St Kevin's Bed. According to legend, the saint retreated here to avoid the amorous wiles of a female demon sent to tempt him. The earliest building in Glendalough, Templenaskellig, the partly reconstructed rectangular 'church of the rock', can only be reached by boat.

KILKENNY (right), an attractive market town on the River Nore, also grew up around an early monastery, founded by St Canice in the 6th century, though the existing St Canice's Cathedral dates from the 13th century. It was badly damaged by Cromwell's troops, who stabled their horses there, and was restored in 1866.

In 1391 Kilkenny Castle was bought by the 3rd Earl of Ormonde, appointed Chief Butler of Ireland by Henry II. Afterwards his heirs took the name of Butler and the family became one of the most important and influential in southern Ireland. The castle, built in the 12th century by William le Mareschal, remained the family seat until the 1930s. A number of family portraits remain in the castle, which now belongs to the city.

At *CARRICK-ON-SUIR*, County Tipperary, a gabled Tudor mansion adjoins the 13th-century keep of another Ormonde Castle (above left). The old castle is one of several claimants to be the birthplace of Anne Boleyn, who was the granddaughter of the 10th Earl of Ormonde. The 10th Earl, 'Black Tom', built the manor house to entertain Elizabeth I and it still contains several busts of the Queen, who never made the expected visit. It has some of Ireland's earliest stucco work and the country's only surviving Elizabethan Long Gallery.

FITZWILLIAM SQUARE (right) is probably the best preserved of Dublin's great Georgian squares, dating from the 1820s. Most of the houses have been turned into consulting rooms, making this Dublin's Harley Street. Other examples of 18th-century architecture line the surrounding streets, but in parts of the city the houses have decayed badly and been turned into tenements.

Merrion Square is lined on three sides by imposing mansions, with attractive door-ways (below) and wrought-iron work, built by John Ensor for the estate of Lord Fitzwilliam of Meryon. Sir William and Lady Wilde, parents of Oscar, once lived here, as did W.B.Yeats and the judge and diarist Sir Jonah Barrington. On the west side of the square is Leinster Lawn, where the statues of the railway tycoon William Dargan and George Bernard Shaw stand outside the National Gallery; Dargan's money funded the collection and Shaw left the gallery a third of his estate.

TRINITY COLLEGE, one of the city's most handsome buildings, has a 91 m (300 ft) Palladian facade, dating from the 1750s, by the London architects John Sanderson and Henry Keene. Also from the 18th century are the chapel and examination hall, or theatre, both designed by Sir William Chambers, with excellent stucco work by Michael Stapleton. The huge gilt chandelier in the theatre came from the old House of Commons on College Green. The famous library, begun in 1712, has a Long Room extending 60 m (197 ft), lined with marble busts and with a barrel-vaulted roof added in Victorian times. The gem of its collection is the illuminated manuscript of the **Book of Kell**s, dating from around AD 800.

LEINSTER HOUSE, now used as the parliament building, was designed in the style of a country house for the Earl of Kildare in 1745; Washington's White House was built to a similar plan.

INDEX

Page numbers in **italic** refer to the illustrations

Abbot's Bromley, 103
Abergavenny, 70
Adam, Robert, 108, 130-4
Albert, Prince Consort, 15, 17, 170-1
Albert Memorial, *15*
Aldeburgh, 109
Alnwick, 129, 130, *140*
Alum Bay, 33
Anglesey, 75
Antrim, *189*
Aran Islands, 193, *194-5*
Arley Hall, Cheshire, 162
Aros Castle, 175
Arthur, King, 48, 53, 76, 82, 171
Artro, River, *78*, 83
Atherstone, 103
Audley End, Essex, *108*
Augusta, Queen, 18
Avebury, 48
Aviemore, 182
Avon, River, 92-7

Ballachulish, 178
Balmoral, 170
Bamburgh Castle, *143*
Bardsey Island, 77
Barnhill, *175*
Bath, *50*
Battersea Power Station, *17*
Battle, 28
Beachy Head, 30, 38
Beara, 201
Becket, St Thomas á, 36
Beddgelert, 82
Bede, Venerable, 129, 164
Belfast, 198
Ben Bulben, *193*
Berkeley Castle, *89*
Bevan, Aneurin, 80
Bibury, 103
Bideford, 59
Big Ben, *11*
Birinus, St, 21
Birmingham, 89
Bisham, *21*
Black Mountains, *66-7*, 70
Blackmore, R. D., 48, 53
Blackpool, 151
Blaenau Ffestiniog, *81*
Blakeney Point, 113
Bodiam Castle, *28*

Bodmin Moor, 50, 53, *62*
Bognor Regis, 34
Boleyn, Anne, 12, 203
Book of Kells, 190, 204
Border Country, 168
Borrowdale, *154*
Boughton House, Northants, 91
Bourton-on-the-Water, *92*
Bradford-on-Avon, *51*
Bramall Hall, Greater Manchester, 155
Brecon Beacons , *72-3*, 75
Bridge of Sighs, Cambridge, *115*
Brighton, *32*, 33
Broads, The, 111-12
Broadway Tower, *98*
Brompton Oratory, *15*
Brown, Lancelot 'Capability', 33, 108, 134
Brympton d'Evercy, *53*
Burnham Beeches, 21
Burns, Robert, 168-70
The Burren, 195
Burton, Richard, 80
Bury St Edmunds, 123
Buttermere, *160*
Buttertubs, *134*

Cader Idris, 82
Cadnam, 45
Caernarfon Castle, *78*
Caerphilly Castle, *74*
Caesar, Julius, 26, 28
Cairngorms, 182
Caldey, 85
Cambridge, 111, *115*
Canary Wharf, *10*
Cannock Chase, 89
Canterbury Cathedral, *36-7*, 39
Cardiff, 74
Carrick-on-Suir, County Tipperary, *203*
Carroll, Lewis, 22
Castle Howard, Yorkshire, 134
Castlerigg Stone Circle, *154*
Castletown Bearhaven, 201
Celts, 189-90
Chalk, Kent, *34*
Chambers, Sir William, 18, 19, 204
Charles, Prince of Wales, 72, 78
Charles I, King, 18, 171
Chartwell, Kent, *41*
Chatham, 41
Chatsworth, Derbyshire, *105*
Cherhill Down, *59*

Chesil Bank, 57
Chesterfield, *96*
Cheviots, 126, 130
Chillingham, 130
Chilterns, 17-19, *21*
Cholmondeley Castle, Cheshire, 162
Churchill, Sir Winston, 10, 41
Cinque Ports, 28-32
Cissbury Ring, *43*
Clapham, Yorkshire, *137*
Clonmacnois, County Offaly, 190
Clovelly, *57*
Coalbrookdale, 101
Coalport, 101
Colchester, 111, 123
Columba, St, 193
Constable, John, 108, 112
Cook, Captain, 143
Cookham, 15-17
Cork, *200-1*
Cotehele House, Cornwall, *63*
Cotswolds, 86, 89
Cotterstock, 91
Coventry Cathedral, 102-3
Crabbe, George, 108-9
Crewkerne, *53*
Crickhowell, 70
Crome, John, 108
Cromwell, Oliver, 28, 89, 94, 195, 199, 203
Cromwell's Castle, 65
Cuckmere Haven, 30
Culbone Church, *49*
Culloden Moor, *182*

Dan-yr-Ogof caves, 72
Darby, Abraham, 101
Dargan, William, 204
Dartmoor, *60-1*
Dartmouth, 59
Deal, *26*, 32
Dean Village, Edinburgh, *172*
deer, *179*
Derwentwater, *146-7*
Dickens, Charles, 35, 38-9, 57
Doonagore, *195*
Dorchester, Oxfordshire, 21
Dove Cottage, Cumbria, *158*
Dover, 32
Dozmary Pool, 53
Dragon Hill, *24*
Drake, Sir Francis, 59
Drumcliff, 193
Du Maurier, Daphne, 50-3, 201

Dublin, 198, **204**
Duddington, **91**
Duddon, River, **162**
Duich, Loch, **177**
Dunboy Castle, 201
Dundrennan Abbey, 169
Dunluce Castle, **189**
Durdle Door, 54
Durham, 129, **139**

East Bergholt, 112
East Lulworth, 54
Edinburgh, **172-3**
Edward, Black Prince, 36
Edward I, King, 72, 78, 91
Eggardon Hill, **46-7**
Eildon Hills, 171
Eilean Donan Castle, **177**
Elan Valley, **76-7**
Elizabeth I, Queen, 89, 152, 169, 203
Ellesmere Port, **148**
Ely Cathedral, **120-1**
Epping Forest, **109**
Eton College, 15
Exmouth, **57**

Farndale, 141
Fens, The, **122**
Ffestiniog railway, 81
Forest of Bowland, 151
Forest of Dean, 92
Fotheringhay, 91
Framlingham Castle, **113**

Gainsborough, Thomas, 108
Galashiels, 168
Gap of Dunloe, 199
Geddington, 91
George III, King, 18, 19, 57, 108
George IV, King, 10, 18, 33
George V, King, 33-4
Glanmore Lake, **201**
Glastonbury Tor, 53
Glen More Forest Park, 182
Glen Shiel, **177**
Glencoe, **180-1**
Glendalough, **203**
Goodrich Castle, 94
Gortahork, **186-7**
Gower Peninsula, **74**, 75
Grasmere, 158
Gray, Thomas, 97, 158
Great Langdale, 163
Great Skellig, 199

Grenville, Sir Richard, 59
Grisedale, **157**

Haddon Hall, Derbyshire, **102-3**
Hadrian's Wall, 129, **144-5**
Hardy, Thomas, 50
Harris, **185**
Heacham, **123**
Hebrides, 185
Helvellyn, 157
Helm Crag, **159**
Henley-on-Thames, 17
Henry II, King, 18, 36
Henry III, King, 12, 18
Henry IV, King, 12, 36, 115
Henry VII, King, 36
Henry VIII, King, 18, 32, 41, 72
Hereford Cathedral, 102
High Street, 164
Highlands, 170-80
Hilda, St, **130**
Holy Island, 129, **143**
hops, 35
Horsey Mere, **106-7**
Hound Tor, **60-1**
Housesteads, 144
The Hurlers, **62**

Inishmore, **194**
Ironbridge Gorge Museum, 101
Isle of Wight, 33, 34

James I, King, 10, 172
Jedburgh, 168
Jodrell Bank telescope, **149**
John, Augustus, 80
John, King, 15, 97, 123, 152
Joseph of Arimathea, 53-7

Kenilworth Castle, 89
Kevin, St, 203
Kew Gardens, **18-19**
Kew Palace, 19
Kilfenora, 195
Kilkenny, **203**
Kilpeck, **94**
King's Cliffe, 91
King's College, Cambridge, **115**
King's Lynn, **120**
Kinlochleven, 178
Kinnock, Neil, 80
Kipling, Rudyard, 39-41
Kirby Hall, Northamptonshire, 91
Kirkcudbright, **168-9**

Knole, Kent, 32
Kyrle, John, 93

Lake District, 146, 148-51, 157-64
Lancaster, **152**
Langdale Pikes, 163
Lansdowne Column, **59**
Lavenham, **117**
Lawrence, T. E., 80
Layer Marney Tower, **111**
Leamaneagh Castle, **195**
Leamington Spa, 89
Leane, Lough, **198**, 199
Leeds, **129**
Leinster House, Dublin, 204
Leven, Loch, **178**
Lewis, Island of, **184-5**
Lincolnshire Wolds, **124**
Lindisfarne Castle, **143**
Lingmoor Fell, **163**
Linlithgow Palace, **171**
Lisburn, 193
Lisdoonvarna, 195
Lissadell House, 193
Little Moreton Hall, Cheshire, **148**, 155
Little Skellig, **199**
Liverpool, **151**
Llanbedr, 78
Llandanwg, **83**
Llandudno, 75
Llangynrdr, 70
Llanthony Priory, **68**
Lleyn Peninsula, 77, 80
Lloyd George, David, 80
London, 10-15
Londonderry, Marchioness of, 190-1
Lower Slaughter, 92
Lulworth Cove, 54
Lulworth Skipper, **54**
Lune Valley, 137
Lutyens, Sir Edwin, 33, 143, 151
Lyndhurst, 45
Lytham St Anne's, 151

Malham Cove, **132-3**
Malham Tarn, **132**
Malvern Hills, 92
Manchester, 151
Mark Ash, **44-5**
Martindale, 164
Mary, Queen of Scots, 91, 169, 171-2
Mellifont Abbey, 190
'Merry Maidens', St Buryan, 50

INDEX

Minsmere, 113
Minstead, 45
Moher, Cliffs of, **195**
Morecambe Bay, 151
Mount Stewart, County Down, **190-1**
Muckross Abbey, 198

Naunton, **86-7**
The Needles, **33**
Needle's Eye, **129**
Ness, Loch, **166-7**
Ness Gardens, Cheshire, 162
New Forest, **44-5**
Newby Hall, Yorkshire, 130-4
Nidderdale, 141
Norton Priory, Cheshire, 161-2
Nymans, Sussex, **42**

Oare Water Valley, **48**
Offa's Dyke, 68
Oldbury Castle, **59**
Orkneys, 179
Orwell, George, 175
Overy Staithe, **118-19**
Oxford, **22**

Palm House, Kew Gardens, **18-19**
Pangbourne, 17
pargeting, **117**
Patrick, St, 190
Paxton, Sir Joseph, 18, 105
Peak District, 92, 105
Pen-y-Fan, 72
Pendle Hill, 152
Pennines, 126
Penrhyn Castle, **81**
Percy family, 140
Plas Newydd, **85**
Plymouth, 59
Polesden Lacey, Surrey, **38-9**
Poul-an-ionain, 195
Pooley Bridge, 164
Portrush, 189
Portsmouth, 41
Potter, Beatrix, 157
Poulinabrone, 195
Putney, **17**

Radcliffe Camera, Oxford, **22**
Raleigh, Sir Walter, 59
Richard II, King, 11, 28
Richborough, 28
Richmond, Yorkshire, **134**
Richmond Hill, 8

Robert the Bruce, 190
Robin Hood's Bay, 141-3
Rockbourne, 45
Ross Castle, 199
Ross-on-Wye, **93**
Royal Navy, 41
Ruskin, John, 148-51
Rydal Mount, 158
Rye, **29**

St Catherine's Island, **84-5**
St Finbarr's Cathedral, Cork, **200**
St Govan's Chapel, **76**
St Paul's Cathedral, **12**
Salehurst, **35**
Saling Hall, **111**
Scarborough, 131, 141
Scilly Isles, 65
Scotney Castle, Kent, **41**
Scott, Sir Giles Gilbert, 17, 151
Scott, Sir Walter, 85, 168, 171
Scott's View, **171**
Seven Sisters, **30**
Severn, River, 97, **97**, 101
Shap Abbey, 164
Shaw, George Bernard, 190-3, 204
Shetlands, 179
Shingle Street, **117**
Skellig Michael, 199
Smardale Viaduct, **161**
Snowdonia National Park, 75-6, **82-3**
Snowshill, **89**
Somersby, 124
South Downs, 34-8
Spencer, Stanley, 15-17
Spey, River, **182-3**
Standing Stones of Callanish, **185**
Stokesay Castle, **98-9**
Stonehenge, 48, **59**
Stourhead, Wiltshire, **48**
Stratford-upon-Avon, 89, 97
Swaledale, **137**, 141
Symonds Yat, **94**, 97
Synge, J. M., 190, 194

Tatton Park, Cheshire, 161
Tenby, 80, 85
Tennyson, Alfred Lord, 124
Thames Barrier, 10, **10**
Thames Valley, 8-25
Thomas, Dylan, 80
Tintagel, 53
Tintern Abbey, **68**
Tithe Barn, Bradford-on-Avon, **51**

Tobermory, **174-5**
Tower of London, **12**
Tresco, 65
Triangular Lodge, Northants, **98**
Trinity College, Cambridge, 115
Trinity College, Dublin, 204
Tynemouth Priory, **139**

Uffington Castle, **24**
Ullswater, 157
Ulpha, 162
Upper Slaughter, 92
Usk, 70
Usk Valley, **70-1**

Vale of the White Horse, **24**
Vanbrugh, Sir John, 108, 130, 134
Vernon, Dorothy, 102
Victoria, Queen, 15, 18, 34, 109, 170
Vindolanda, 144

Warkworth, **140**
Warwick, 97
Wayland's Smithy, 24
Wells Cathedral, **51**
Wensleydale, 141
West Dean, 30
Westminster, Palace of, 10, 11
Westminster Hall, **11**
Whitby Abbey, **130**
Wicken Fen, **122-3**
Wilde, Oscar, 193, 204
William the Conqueror, 12, 18, 28,
    45, 68-72, 97
Willy Lott's Cottage, **112**
Windsor Castle, 15, 18
Winnats Pass, **105**
Wistman's Wood, **60**
Worcester Cathedral, **96-7**, 102
Wordsworth, William, 68, 85, 148,
    158, 163
Worms Head, **74**
Wren, Sir Christopher, 11, 12
Wye, River, **94**, 97

Yeats, W.B., 190, 193, 204